SABATO

The Untold Story

Second Edition

BY

ANTONIO SABATO, Jr.

With Co Author

TONY MOORE

ISBN **979-8-218-37970-4** Paperback Sabato the Untold Story
Second Edition

This book was printed in the United States of America

SABATO

The Untold Story

Second Edition

Cover photo compliments Jason Ellis Photography

jasonellisphoto@yahoo.com

Thank you for purchasing my book. I hope you love reading it as much as I loved living it!

Table of Contents

Foreword

By Co-Author

Tony Moore

In writing Antonio's book, I got to know him, probably as much as anyone could know another person while writing about their life and all they achieved. What struck me, as I hope it will for you too, is the resilience and honesty of Antonio Sabato Jr. and his family, his love for his family and how he remained unchanged with everything that had happened to him and his family.

Antonio, is one of the hardest working, honest and most resilient people I have ever had the pleasure to meet. Nothing stops him from his intent to succeed and as you read his story, I think you will agree as well. It is his drive to succeed that has led him to come out of being blacklisted by Hollywood, to move on to do what he loves, making his movies his way.

Writing Antonio's story inspired me to co-found Briton Publishing LLC, in order to get *Sabato the Untold Story* to the public. This was our first book published.

In this second edition we included some beautiful photographs of Antonio's family as well as photos containing a record of Antonio's 30-year career working with and meeting some of the most famous people of the present time.

It has been a pleasure to write Antonio Sabato, Jr.'s story and we sincerely hope you love reading our book.

Chapter 1

Why I Ran for Congress

People have asked me why I left a perfectly good career in movies to change direction and run for Congress. The truth is, that I saw a growing disconnect between me and my position of constant and well-paid work, which I loved, compared to what I was seeing as a situation getting worse and worse in Hollywood and in southern California.

It was, in no small part, seeing the homelessness that I saw growing, seemingly at an exponential rate from when my family moved to Hollywood in 1985 and what I began to see developing towards 2016 when I ran for Congress.

I asked many questions talking with local leaders as to what was going to happen with these thousands of homeless people and the answer was always the same, "Who knows!" But for me it seemed there was plenty of money available in Los Angeles with thousands of well-off companies, Hollywood's billions and a very rich community when we moved there. So, it made me ask, "where has the money gone?" One figure I saw reported at that time was a $75 billion surplus of cash in the California State coffers. Why was it not used to set up shelters?

Compared to now, there is no comparison, not only with the increasing homelessness but also with increased crime. I felt I had to at least try to do something to change this unacceptable "status quo" with all I saw, with no change in sight.

I also saw that a continuous leadership, from one side of the aisle, had been responsible for decades, running California, yet nothing had changed. In fact, what did change was that things were getting worse. Part of the problem was the climbing cost of housing where thousands of residents could no longer afford their homes there. But I am one of those people who cannot ignore this and turn a blind eye to it to be one of the "silent majority."

So, in 2016, I switched and went into politics to try my best at changing what I saw with billions of dollars being available but none of that money being used to improve things for Californians and especially those homeless people living on the Los Angeles streets.

Making the move to politics cost me, who knows how much, in the form of movie work that I had to turn down while I was focused on running for Congress. I couldn't take on any acting roles while I was campaigning. It's hard to estimate just how much I lost in movies I had already been cast in, because of my decision to run for Congress. But that, as they say, is water under the bridge now. The total cost of the campaign plus losing work, is not easily calculated and now, as you will see, I'm moving on to better things.

There were several campaign management companies that offered to "help" but with no guarantees of success and believe me they were very expensive. I was told they were specialists in campaign management something I was not an expert at. They spent a lot of the money I had raised on things that, in my opinion, did not lead to more votes for me. As a result, I was less than impressed with what they did for me in my campaign.

I am not blaming them at all for my failure to win, but in retrospect, I can honestly say they did a mediocre job at best. However, they did a brilliant job at coming after me for their bonuses after my campaign failed, for what in my opinion they did little to earn. I paid their fees out of my own pocket and as I was to learn there is apparently a bonus for failing!

My opponent didn't even live in the county she was running in, which was the 26th district. To me this should have been a bigger issue for those voting for her, but apparently, according to the stated results, it wasn't and she refused to debate me on live TV.

My campaign was run on unity, improving things for the community but that didn't gain the traction that I had hoped for. I really wanted to bring California back to where it was when I first moved there in 1985.

Did I Make a Difference?

I still ask myself; *Did I make a difference?* I believe I did, even though I didn't win. I believe I was a forerunner for change and hopefully I started something which may eventually make a difference not only there in California, but across the entire country. Time will tell, as to how much voters will endure increased violence, paying the highest taxes with increased homelessness, before coming to the realization that they need to change how they vote. As I am writing this, hundreds of thousands of people have left California preferring to live in a State that is run for the benefit of the people not the benefit for the Governor.

There was a general sense of acceptance surrounding a vote for more of the same from the Californian Democrat leadership, which to me, had consistently failed to make a positive difference for ordinary residents in California and especially in Los Angeles.

Last time I looked there are now more than 59,000 homeless in L.A. who are mostly Californians. Yet money was made available to fund low-income housing or affordable housing so where did it all go? I have also been asked would I run again and the answer is no I would not. Not for the obvious reasons you would imagine but also for my family who suffered the entire time.

I wonder how the residents feel now with the spread of unrest, growing crime and increased homelessness caused by the same leaders who have been running things into the ground there for decades.

Apparently, they still want to blame others for their decades-long bad decisions. Their failure, to bring California back to where it was when I first moved there in 1985, is theirs alone to shoulder.

I would not run again, but not for the obvious reasons you would imagine, but for my family who suffered the entire time. A political campaign takes its toll not only on the candidate, but on the entire family.

Because of our political views, based on our past experiences my family and I were relentlessly verbally attacked while we were living in California. They suffered for simply being my family because I supported a presidential candidate who also wanted to make a difference. To me, at that time, support for the opposition was a vote for more of the same and I chose not to be part of this silent majority who complain but do nothing about it.

It was when I agreed to give a speech for the Republican National Congress in Cleveland, that my 30-year career was over and that was the biggest surprise to me. Being *Blacklisted*. was the beginning on the next chapter in my life.

This is what led us, like many others, to move out of the state and my family has never looked back.

Doing what we feel is important, despite the silent majority, can have severe consequences.

Chapter 2

Blacklisted

My family's history, told here in my book, will tell you of my great-grandparents, exterminated in the infamous death camps at Auschwitz, my grandmother, murdered after visiting us in Rome. It was believed by those who knew her, that the socialists did this, when she returned to Prague after they failed to use her to bring my mother, Yvonne, to return there from our home in Italy. Though for what purpose she was murdered we cannot guess, but whatever it was it was a heinous crime against an old lady. Was this again to get my mother to go to her funeral?

My mother was held as a child hostage in Prague, all alone at age eight, for almost a year to ensure her mother and father returned to Prague after being forced to work in Poland, to earn money just to send it all back to the socialist government.

We also lost everything we owned in an arson attack in my family home in Rome, Italy, before finally making it here in America. I worked for 30 years in the Hollywood movie industry, only to see my career brought to an abrupt halt, for speaking with a conservative point of view!

My father, Antonio Sabato, Sr. was a famous movie star in Italy with 60 films to his credit, he was forced to look elsewhere for work when the Italian movie industry all but dried up in the 70s and 80s.

We then had to leave all we had ever known in Italy, where I was born, for a new life here in America. All was going well for me and my family but after I was asked to speak at the Republican National Congressional Committee in 2016, my career ended.

It doesn't matter how famous you are as an actor or actress, how many fans you have or how many millions you have made for Hollywood, with your box office success over a life-long career, having a conservative point of view in today's Hollywood and speaking about it will end your career no matter who you are.

This outcome is not only about me but also for many others in Hollywood who are also blacklisted for being conservatives or for speaking out against the casting couch inner workings of Hollywood.

Working in Hollywood for me and for many others, has become impossible. So how does this work? It works through the network of producers, directors, casting and distributors refusing to cast, fund or distribute films with blacklisted actors.

This is not only about me and the end of my Hollywood based movie career, but it is also about what is going on, behind the scenes in Hollywood, looking only from the outside, watching the actors and actresses, we enjoy watching in a myriad of Hollywood made films and TV shows. These films and TV shows are now sold throughout the entire world from this multi-billion-dollar global industry.

Working in Hollywood for me and for many others, has now become impossible after being blacklisted. So how does this work? It works with the producers, directors, casting and distributors refusing to cast, fund or distribute films with politically blacklisted actors.

In my case I made 90 movies and TV shows, enjoyed by millions of my fans, but my run for Congress in 2016 resulted in me never working again, a decision made by those few who have made certain that careers like mine are ended as well as being ended for other conservative actors and actresses, like me, who dare to speak about it.

This can happen not only for talking about our conservative political views, but it can also happen to all the actresses for daring to speak out against being sexually assaulted in the infamous "Casting Couch" mentality, that seems to be the accepted norm. Again, this is only within certain factions in Hollywood as there are also many in casting, producing and directing who are not like this. Let's be clear, I know many will say, "it takes two to tango," but does that change the fact? Does that make it OK to put actresses in such an impossible position in order to get work?

This is made worse by the silent majority of those who know this is the case because preventing people from working is a widely known fact within Hollywood. Yet despite knowing what's going on, they continue to say nothing and in doing so, they silently condone this behavior and allow it to continue. They are forced to do this if they want the work, so speaking out is a no-no.

Our right to free speech and the 1st Amendment, in the "Land of the Free," should be protected at all costs and not traded off for a code of silence. But when it comes to a corrupt system, like Hollywood, people have to accept it if they want to work in that movie industry.

This is not about the vast majority of good directors, hard-working crew members or actors and actresses, many of whom I have had the pleasure to work with, who are also part of Hollywood. Most of these are honest hard-working stagehands, or people working with the technical side of this business, people who I love their work and they are the salt of the earth!

Running as a Republican for Congress in 2016 was far worse for me than anything I had been through before coming to America as you will read here, further on, in my book.

My family had to flee from socialist run Czechoslovakia to Italy, then having to leave Italy, where I was born, because there was no money for the luxury of making Italian films then in Italy. It was also the many Hollywood films that were flooding the world market forcing the Italian made movie industry to dry up.

As if that wasn't bad enough, the devastating fire in our home in Rome, when I was eight-years old which, according to the fire chief at the scene, in a conversation with my mother, was started by an incendiary bomb that was set deliberately placed in our home. We lost everything we had ever owned in that fire and had to start over again, with nothing but the clothes on our backs. Who was it that did this? We will never know. My dad was an actor, my mom was a hard-working mother and we were just children when it happened. All fingers point to those in power in the then socialists in Czechoslovakia.

So, we emigrated to America in 1985, when I was 13 years-old, which by the way, took us five years and tens of thousands of dollars to accomplish legally. Now after living the dream and doing what I love to do, my agents, casting directors and producers will not book me for future work. Even the web is biased with articles and slanted news articles going against blacklisted actors and conservatives.

But what is going on today in Hollywood has also affected many other actors and actresses who have also been blacklisted not only for expressing their right to freedom of speech but worse still, for actresses, who have come forward telling of sexual abuse and even sexual assault by these same movie moguls who then blacklist them for speaking out. Is this the America I left Italy for? These are both forms of abuse in the workplace.

My agent, someone who I have worked with for many years, told me in our last conversation back in 2016, that the work we had already lined up was not now going ahead after I had been previously cast in upcoming films and TV shows. That work I had already landed would have kept me busy for around three years, in shows and TV work, but now it was all gone.

There was one casting director though who did give me work after we contacted each other through Linked-In, of all places, when I was so desperate for work. I had placed a request on Linked In to find work. She was casting for a new movie called *"One Nation Under God."* I landed that role as the result of the casting director's belief that I could play that part based on my acting and nothing to do with politics. Since then, Scott Baio, who is a registered Republican and who campaigned for Reagan, along with a Christian faith-based, production company also found me work.

Many actors and actresses who have, at some point, in interviews, on TV shows and in the media, spoken out and have told us that blacklisting is widespread. But they are far fewer than the many other actors who are too afraid to speak out as I have for fear of reprisals. But many also may share a conservative view in private as they have said so to me but can never say in public that they are conservatives. They become part of the "Hollywood club" even if privately they don't agree. The silent majority is the biggest force against freedom and the First Amendment.

But being prevented from ever working again, in an industry we may have been in for 30 years should never be acceptable to any of us, especially when actors winning Oscars can voice their opinions in their widely televised acceptance speeches, seen by millions, expressing their Liberal views or expressing their hatred for an elected president with impunity and with loud applause.

They do this merely to show they are in the Hollywood club, this "behind the scenes" socialist club, of decision makers who will continue to allow actors to work, because they are "In." This club exists to control who is allowed to work and who is banned, regardless of their skill or popularity. Many of those who spout their liberal views don't even believe what they are saying but they show the "club" they are liberal. This goes to the very heart of the corruption they represent, whether it's the casting couch or our political views.

What is going on in America right now should be unacceptable to everyone. This is how every socialist and communist regime throughout history has started, by creeping into what were once thriving societies, in Czechoslovakia, Venezuela and other places like Lithuania, Latvia and Estonia. It begins with gradually limiting free speech against conservatism, while only accepting a Liberal/socialist viewpoint, represented by the far left in the Democrat party.

Biased Media

It moves into the schools and colleges indoctrinating our children and teens through a biased education system. Is this what we now have here? You may say, "This could never happen here" but, this is happening right here and right now and I am proof of this. The control of the media, limiting free speech and limiting the education for our children are key components for regime change to take hold. Just look around you and see if this is not true right now. Of all main-stream news outlets, barely one channel (Newsmax) now shows a conservative but balanced view. The once trusted network news programs are now little more than biased mouthpieces, propaganda, for socialism and their statements are exhorting their extreme left-wing policies.

We are seeing this now not only in the main- stream news media, but also in the social media of Facebook, Twitter (now X), Google and YouTube to name just a few, they are openly blocking blogs and tweets, as well as de-monetizing conservative media, which they say goes against their policies. This is blatant censorship across social media without ever telling us what those policies are.

Jesse Walker, who has written articles for *The New York Times, The Wall Street Journal* and *The Washington Post,* wrote in September 2018, that as he saw it, *"There is an organized effort to remove people from the movie industry for their political opinions."* And he's right!

It started in Germany, leading up to World War II, with anti-government statements in the press and with the "Brown Shirt" gangs on the streets, protesting ultra-high inflation but by the time academia, the middle class and the then, silent majority realized what was happening, it was too late to stop it.

Censorship often ends with either a dictatorship, socialism or communism and when that happened in all the socialist countries, as my family saw first-hand, it led to disaster and mass "people control" with little to no freedom of speech. All were affected who allowed it to happen despite which view they had, left or right.

Italy, my original home, the country of Ferrari, Fashion, good wine, and ancient history, does not compare with what it was in the 60's and 70's and has been under a socialist leadership for decades.

At the time of writing this according to *Heritage.org*, Italy is ranked thirty-sixth among forty-four countries in the European region. Its overall score, measured across many fronts and economic factors, is below the regional average, a far cry from the glory that was Rome.

Why was the Berlin Wall destroyed? Why did Czechoslovakia's ordinary hard-working people, many of whom were family friends, rise-up against socialism's one-party system in their Velvet Revolution of 1989? Why did 2 million people join hands linking Latvia, Estonia and Lithuania, in what was called, "The Baltic Way" a 600 km (450 mile) line of linked hands in protest against socialism.

Prosperity and freedom and the right to free speech, which is everything America stands for, or certainly used to, is now at risk and personified in places like Hollywood, who are charging ahead through our social media, to create a socialist based movie industry. Do they not realize that if this country becomes socialist, under any other name, "Democrat" or "Liberal" their industry is finished because far fewer people could afford the luxury to go to the movies.

A poll carried out by *The Washington Post*, published recently by PEW Research, showed some twenty-three major news channels, news and media publications which were named on their chart; including the *BBC, CNN, MSNBC, PBS, NPR*, most were left wing biased and only seven were conservative. Of those seven, only *Fox News,* at the time of the poll, was conservative leaning and was a main-stream news channel with name recognition similar to those mentioned above.

This is not the case now however since Fox has now joined the ranks of the more Democrat leaning supporters, even firing it's most vocal and most popular host Tucker Carlson. So, what conclusion should we come to, when most Americans are getting their facts from this spread of socialist and left-wing biased news and media propaganda?

When I ran for congress, it was because of what my family had been through in Czechoslovakia and Italy and what I was now seeing right here in America and particularly, in California. Perhaps we should just keep quiet and say nothing to keep earning a living. But if we all do, keep quiet, is this the America we all want? Do we want a media that is more and more biased and more powerful, while only airing one point of view, pushing their one-sided socialist agenda? One thing is for certain, if we all do, in fact keep quiet, America will be a socialist country in our lifetime.

You may think, on reading my story that I am exaggerating what I now see happening here in the U.S., but my family has seen this, "conversion from freedom," first-hand and now we are seeing the beginning of this right here in America.

Kowtow To the Few in Power

If we do not speak out who will? All who want to work in Hollywood, have to "kowtow" to the wishes of a few in positions of power and who have abused their power, by blacklisting others, solely for not sharing the same political views they do. If it was a general condition to not talk about politics fine then that would work for both left and right, but this only censors one side and not the other.

This happens in private meetings, a small group of people who regularly meet to decide on leading actors, directors and producers for upcoming projects. It may take only one person in that group to vote no for that potential actor not to be cast. Those who have conservative views and who speak about them will not be given work! Maybe a private list is circulated, or maybe a watch group there to monitor and censure those of us who are conservative, or those actresses who report being sexually assaulted in this elitist and corrupt industry and in doing so risk themselves to become blacklisted?

This is a very slippery slope into something we should all be genuinely concerned about regardless of your views on politics. If censorship is allowed for one party or group, it undermines the very fabric of our society. How did Hollywood move from McCarthyism, hunting for communists in the 40's and 50's to be now hunting conservatives in the present day? What or more importantly who caused this change?

The choice of who would be best for a part should be purely based on their fit for the role and their box office success, that justifies their huge salaries based on their popularity and acting ability. That choice should not be based on which political party they prefer.

We emigrated to America in 1985, when I was 13 years-old, which by the way, took us five years and tens of thousands of dollars to accomplish legally. Now after doing what I love to do, my Hollywood based agents, casting directors and producers will not book me for future work.

The silent majority throughout history have done nothing but have allowed censorship to grow, are those who have always realized, when it is too late, the devastation that has happened to their country through socialism.

Chapter 3

History Repeated

On June 22, 1950, a pamphlet entitled "Red Channels" was published. It focused on the broadcasting industry and it identified 151 entertainment industry professionals who, it alleged back then, were "Reds, Fascists, Communists and their sympathizers," soon, most of those named, along with a host of other artists, were barred from employment in most of the entertainment field. They were alleged to be communist sympathizers and socialists.

Jesse Walker, wrote in September 201 and, explained that as he saw it, "There is an organized effort to remove people from the movie industry for their political opinions."

He also said, "Anyone who cares about freedom of expression should object to censorship by proxy, how it came about back in the early days of the cold war and as it now threatens to re-emerge in social media today." And he is dead right it is happening right now! History is repeating itself anti-Semitism is happening right here right now in America and in Europe and after we lost 75 million lives to destroy the Nazi regime. The same regime that took my great grandparents' lives in Auschwitz along with six million other Jews.

#MeToo Movement

Our right to work, to speak freely and to support whoever we want to run our country, through a fair and unbiased transparent voting system, without losing our livelihood as a result. Free speech must be protected by law, but as I have found free speech has consequences.

Proof of this is the recent trial of Harvey Weinstein and the #MeToo movement who collectively decided to end his oppressive behavior. Would there be enough people who have been blacklisted to come together to force a change through an alternative to Hollywood, funding films with a free cast given the work based on their collective ability, success and fit for the part, not based on their political persuasion.

Throughout history, action is only taken when it is too late and I'm under no illusion that this would be a difficult undertaking but at least through my own story I'm highlighting what happened not only to myself but also to so many other good people whose very livelihoods are being controlled by what they can say, what they can openly think and what is acceptable to a very few people who control whether others, like us, can ever work again in the industry we love.

In all those countries I have mentioned, Poland, Czechoslovakia, Hungary, Italy, places where my family have seen the results of socialism, dictatorship or communism firsthand and are now seeing this begin here in the U.S. under a more acceptable label "Liberalism," or Democrat, we see we are facing the same potential for history to repeat itself right here, in the land of the free.

Now, we can see that the majority of young people want to change America into what they see as a more liberal country. Is this the product of a failed educational system, with an agenda of false history now taught by our many liberal thinking teachers? As if this wasn't bad enough, do we have the additional input of the relentlessly, liberally biased, press? Many American schools now do not teach about World War 2 thus refusing to teach our children about the hatred of one-man Adolf Hitler to cause a holocaust leading to more than 6 million Jews to be exterminated and 75 million more who also died trying to stop him. Was this not a world event worth teaching to prevent it happening again?

In my view this starts with our school system failing to teach our children, who are the future of this country, failing to teach what socialism, dictatorship and communism are truly about. Failing to teach this, now unpopular truth, about how this has been tried in other countries where socialism has consistently failed, leaves them all believing the lies they are hearing from the biased press that now dominates the American news and the "social" media. We are even seeing a re-emergence of those who believe the Earth is flat! Is this the product of an effective education system?

Why would any country want open borders, allowing criminals or anyone with any nefarious personal agenda into their country? Some are truly refugees, but this has to be established through laws and effective border controls to find this out before they can be given asylum.

The loss of America's identity while ignoring parts of the original Declaration of Independence, free speech and allowing open borders, a biased press printing propaganda not news, with blacklisting which goes directly against freedom of speech, as I have tried to show here. This must never be allowed to gain momentum.

If we decide to act, together, to speak out, to change something that is wrong, we can succeed! America is proof of this.

Chapter 4

The Silent Majority

Throughout history the silent majority have done nothing but allowed censorship to grow and are those who have always realized, when it is too late, the devastation that has happened to their country through socialism. Will this happen here?

My family has seen and experienced first-hand what socialism, communism and dictatorship-based regimes have done to what were once beautiful and vibrant countries.

Only those of you who are the "Silent Majority," and can see the damage that blacklisting and censorship has done and still is doing to our movie industry, can help to stop this! But as the now famous phrase says, "Just say No" but in this case it is to say no to blacklisting.

Many are apparently, not saying anything by default have accepted to allow fellow actors and actresses, their friends in the same business they are in, to be bullied by the few who have been allowed to do this. Make no mistake, this is bullying. Bullying is not only physical it is mental too. Allowing those who have an apparent power that no one gave them to choose who can work and who can't. This is not based on their box office success or skills as an actor.

The women, of Hollywood's movie industry, have used their power, to make the change, by hitting Hollywood hard where it hurts most, financially! If the silent majority also speak out, we can all make Hollywood what it once was, without the divisive business it has become, in movies, in the news networks and social media. If we can't change Hollywood, maybe we need to create a second version, non-political version, focused purely on making entertaining movies and nothing else.

I know that America is better than this and America needs inclusion and unity and not division, separation and hate. I will make future movies that promote my beliefs as I have started to do.

Right now, as I am writing my book, this is beginning to gain traction in some of main-stream news media and the number of women making allegations against people like Harvey Weinstein, but there is nothing cohesive, or a movement against what pollutes Hollywood.

We are divided right now and not part of a cohesive force to either legally block what is happening financially, or to launch an alternative to Hollywood, that would stop *Blacklisting,* once and for all but this can only change if we, the participants, make it so.

"In a time of deceit telling the truth is a revolutionary act."
—George Orwell

Chapter 5

Best Buddies

In 2019, a charity organization, Best Buddies, which is an international nonprofit organization that has been going for thirty years and is dedicated to ending the social, physical and economic isolation that affects the 200 million people with intellectual and developmental difficulties (IDD).

They sparked criticism when it was announced that I was to be honored by Best Buddies, as their "Hero of Inclusion" at the organization's annual Champion of the Year Gala in Palm Beach, Florida, in November 2019. I have worked with Best Buddies for a very long time and I love what they do, but before this I seldom, if ever spoke about it in public. I am happy to help them in any way I can. But, because I had run my political campaign as a conservative, Best Buddies received criticism for honoring the work we had accomplished together.

Fox News host, Steve Doocy, read an email live on air, in their *Fox & Friends* breakfast show, watched by millions from a major financial contributor to Best Buddies, who withdrew support for Best Buddies over its decision to give me an award. How deep does this go?

That person, whose name was withheld, wrote to the organization saying, "our children must be protected from the garbage that has been elected."

I was invited to respond about this comment so I fired back live on air, to the millions of viewers who watch the *Fox & Friends* breakfast Show.

I addressed the criticism live on *Fox & Friends* on their morning breakfast show, telling them my political opinions have nothing to do with the work I do with Best Buddies. I also told them, "These liberals are out of their minds!" adding, "Just because I support a conservative ideal, you're going to put me down?"

History has shown that left unchecked, these actions become progressively worse. To prevent history repeating itself, this needs to be taken up as a cohesive message through legal, mainstream and social media. Hollywood is not above the law of this land!

When it gets to withdrawing funding for a great humanity-based charity organization, like Best Buddies, who are a non-political charity, things have reached rock bottom!

Chapter 6

Yvonne's Story

My mother, Yvonne Kabouchi Sabato, began performing at just three years old, in Prague, Czechoslovakia, performing with her father's act (see photo). He was riding a monocycle, while balancing on top of a long pole, while an incredibly young Yvonne was doing acrobatics on his shoulders!

However, prior to this, my grandfather, was a chartered accountant and an aristocrat with a thriving business. My grandmother was a well-known seamstress who designed and made high fashion and stage clothing but both were forbidden to continue their work because they refused to join the socialist party. But more about this later.

Their entertainment act became extremely popular with audiences in the beautiful city of Prague. Prague was then and still is a beautiful city with a rich history, in the arts and culture, complete with its stunning architecture. Prague is a city visited by millions of people now. But back then Prague became a socialist run city and ordinary freedoms were banned. Even owning books was banned! *Fahrenheit 451* was a sci-fi movie, written by Ray Bradbury, about the burning of books by a fictitious government of the future, but it was also based on a truth, books were banned in many socialist run countries!

My mother, Yvonne, came originally from English stock and was born with her maiden name Yvonne Williams. Her family history, back in England had the name Saghy.

At three years old Yvonne went on stage taking part in her parents' entertainment act, as a child prodigy, performing her acrobatics. She traveled with her parents' shows and was an integral part of their successful and popular entertainment act.

My grandfather, William Saghy, was originally trained as a certified accountant. He was forced to learn to juggle while riding on his monocycle and he had an immensely popular act back then. For me, he was a very cool grandpa and I am so proud of him!

My grandmother, Magdalena Saghyova, William's wife, was a successful fashion designer and seamstress. I should point out that my grandparents were also *blacklisted* from their original jobs, because they refused to join the new socialist party formed to take control of Czechoslovakia including the beautiful city of Prague where they both lived.

The country changed from being occupied by Nazi's in World War Two, to then then being occupied by Russia, who helped to kick the Nazis out. Russian tanks drove right into Prague and what was thought to be, "saving Czechoslovakia" from the Nazis became yet another occupation.

Russia told the people of Czechoslovakia, that they were saving them from the Nazi's but in fact, they not only marched straight in but then subjugated the people now under socialism. My grandparents were there in Prague and saw all this unfolding first-hand.

A Real-Life Dr. Zhivago Scene

The government even came right into people's homes, like my grandfather's big house and packed complete strangers and families into their houses, with one family per room and all having to share one bathroom.

There was a scene in the beautiful film *Dr. Zhivago,* that showed this very graphically when Zhivago's father, played by Ralph Richardson (as Alexander), went back to his own large home in Russia, after a period of absence, only to find that it was now overrun by communist guards, now occupying his home. They commandeered his house, to place many total strangers inside, so it was now, not his home!

Back then, my grandfather was an aristocrat, because of his job and his public standing, but this made his situation worse with these hateful socialists. As a result, of refusing to join the socialist party, my grandparents were both prevented from continuing with their chosen professions; she, as a successful designer and seamstress and he, as a certified Chartered accountant. To prevent themselves from starvation, as it was impossible to work without a government work permit, they were both forced to learn new skills and so they chose (or it was chosen for them) the entertainment business.

What happened, to cause this betrayal was following a private dinner with "friends," my grandfather who probably had one too many drinks, told his "friends" over the dinner table, he would never join the socialist party. Following that evening, they were told a few days later that the police were coming early the next day at 5 am to arrest my grandfather, for speaking out against joining the socialist party.

They had to act quickly to remove all papers, especially their books and anything that may incriminate them both. All books were banned by the socialists (*Fahrenheit 451* in real life) and they had many, many books. Despite removing all traces of documents and books, he was arrested.

After his arrest, my ever-resourceful grandmother, Magdalena, managed to get papers from her doctor, saying that he was certifiably insane. The document she obtained prevented my grandfather from being imprisoned probably for many years.

Despite being a successful accountant, my grandfather was told he was forbidden to perform his job as an accountant as punishment for not supporting the socialist party. They took away his work permit because he refused to be part of their corruption.

Therefore, he had to learn a new profession and had to discover something else to do, in order to obtain a work permit. He learned a new skill if he was to eat and not starve. A lesson here, controlling work permits as socialists do, will prevent anyone who disagrees with the government from ever having work and thus force them to starvation or join the socialist party. If socialism was so wonderful why did they need to force people to join their party?

He was told he would be a juggler by the socialists who forced their demands on everyone. He did, in turn, learn to become a juggler while riding a monocycle of all things! However, he used his accounting skills to manage their company's books and he took care of their finances.

My grandmother, as I mentioned, also had another skill as a very high-end, well respected and talented seamstress who was known to many people living in Prague. She designed and created beautiful costumes and dresses for the elite and well-known actors and actresses of the day. She created and made beautiful garments that were also worn by models and the elite people in high places.

My grandmother was at the top of her profession back then, but like my grandfather, she too had to learn a new skill if they were to survive. So, she became a dancer and singer.

They both learned these new skills and when they had become proficient enough, they formed their entertainment act, which eventually became their company with my grandmother being a dancer and my grandfather being a unicycling juggler. I have to smile at their resilience in tough times and their ability to reinvent themselves. They say necessity is the mother of invention and as they both proved it was correct as it related to both of them. How relevant this is to me now, with all that is happening to me I am doing what they had to do, reinvent myself.

My mother Yvonne - held as a child hostage.

They traveled to each of the shows in a bus and at night, my then three-year old mother, Yvonne, was hoisted up to sleep on the netting, in the over-head compartment, which was normally used for luggage, but for her it was her bed each night while they were on the road.

Yvonne had to stop working with her family's act as soon as she started school, at age eight as she was already working with them, full-time.

My mother was eight years old in 1955. Czechoslovakia, was now a socialist country and part of Comecon, ruled by Russia. She was forced by the socialist party, to remain in Prague alone, held as a child hostage, while her parents were forced to take their increasingly more popular entertainment act to perform all over Poland. They were part of a cultural exchange, part of a large national theatre representing the Czechoslovakian arts and culture, with ballet dancers, singers, folk dancers and acrobatic acts.

Her mother, my grandmother, wrote many letters to the Prime Minister of Czechoslovakia, asking him to intervene to try to take eight-year-old Yvonne with them on the road to Poland. But no matter how many letters she sent, no one could, or would, help her remain with her parents while they traveled. This was at the height of the cold war and was the socialist's way of ensuring her parents would come back to Prague to be with their daughter.

This went on for almost a year. She was given a ration book for lunch and each day a lady came at night to give her dinner; but she remained at home alone for the entire time while her parents were in Poland.

The daily visit from the "dinner lady," bringing her dinner each evening was mainly to ensure that she remained at home and had not run away. Little Yvonne was not scared during this time because she kept up with her routine of school and ballet lessons every day. As soon as her school had finished, she went off to her ballet lessons and this routine kept her busy every day and helped her to deal with the fact that her parents were away working for almost a year.

She told my sister, Simonne and I about her times alone in Prague and how she spent her time only with adults, not playing with other children, as a normal eight-year-old would do. As she told us, it became normal for her to be busy all the time as that was all she knew.

During all this time my grandmother was allowed only one trip back to Prague to see her daughter, my mother, and to make sure she was alright. But this took considerable pressure from them in order to obtain the necessary travel documents to make the trip without being arrested or maybe even imprisoned, once back in Prague. She knew she could be imprisoned for nothing at all. A common practice in socialist countries is guilty until proven innocent, but never given the chance to defend yourself and how do you prove innocence while in prison?

My mother performed with the top stars in the country and was used to being seen with many famous people in and around Czechoslovakia and especially in the Prague theatrical and music scene.

Miloš Forman

When she was fourteen, she was on stage under the direction of Czech director, Jan Thomas Forman, (Miloš Forman) who was a well-known director in Czechoslovakia. Yvonne and her mother often went dancing with Miloš in the evenings and they got to know each other very well. He gave Yvonne a part in one of his productions, when she was fifteen and she worked with him in the Alhambra theatre as a performer.

Miloš was a very exacting director; a perfectionist and she often told us of the number of times he would make his performers rehearse the same part repeatedly in order for it to be perfect. But she also told us how much fun he was to work with, often doing little things to make them laugh.

It was funny that because of all her ballet and dancing lessons, since she was three years old, the constant training made her feet naturally face outwards, almost in first position whenever she stood still at the microphone.

Every time she stood at the microphone to sing, Miloš kept coming over to her to try to straighten her feet, so they weren't "in the wheat," as he told her, pointing outwards. But as much as he tried, her feet kept pointing outwards. She was singing in Dresden, in Germany, then driving the two hours, with her father to Prague to perform there on the same days as well. Being busy was what she liked; it took her mind away from all she saw under the socialists now leading the country. Yvonne left school at fifteen years old to work in her parents' entertainment company, full-time. She was now a professional on-stage and was also the producer, the choreographer for the dance routines and a ballerina. She was also singing in the shows.

Miloš became an important component of what was known as the Czechoslovakian "New Wave" films. The Czechoslovakian authorities saw his 1967 film, *The Firemen's Ball*, as a hard-hitting and biting satire, based on Eastern European Communism and it was banned for many years, in his home country, Czechoslovakia, as a result.

He left Czechoslovakia emigrating to the U.S.A. and his career soared making such iconic Oscar winning films, *One Flew Over the Cuckoo's Nest.* This film was only the second film to win all five major Academy Awards (Best Picture, Actor in Leading Role, Actress in Leading Role, Director and Screenplay).

Miloš also made the film *Amadeus,* which also gained him an Academy Award for Best Director. He directed *Hair, The People Versus Larry Flynt* and *Man on the Moon.* This proved that suppressing Miloš' talents, under a socialist regime, was reversed when he was given the unrestricted freedom to make award winning movies, here in America, that were enjoyed by millions of people.

Miloš was proof that, under a socialist regime, talent of all kinds, along with natural freedom, is suppressed. How can anyone say this is a good thing? It is not and it is a failed policy that has never worked in any country where it was brought into being by an unsuspecting and ignorant public.

Everyone has talent. What's rare is the courage to follow it to the dark places where it leads. — Erica Jong

Chapter 7

A Murder in Prague

In 1970, my grandmother lived with my mother in Italy but she decided to go back to her original home city, Prague, for a visit and to re-connect with all her many friends there. My mother was twenty-four years old and my sister, Simonne, was then two years old. My mother would not make the trip back to Prague, with her mother because she knew as soon as she entered Czechoslovakia she would be imprisoned or even worse perhaps she would be killed. She knew this for certain following the many threatening letters she received from the Czech authorities.

Towards the end of 1970, it was agreed that my sister would be sent to Prague to spend some time there with her grandmother, but my grandmother said no, not yet as she had a minor surgery procedure there in Prague and suggested the visit be postponed. At the same time, government officials in Prague had been sending my mother many letters asking her to return to Prague. These letters became more demanding, as time went on insisting that she return to Prague.

When my mother tried to marry my father, Antonio Sabato, Sr., when they were both living in Italy, she required some original documents, that were only available from the Prague authorities, to allow her to do this; she needed birth certificates and similar documents that were required to get married in Italy.

She did not yet have an Italian passport and her Czechoslovakian passport had expired. The Czech authorities refused to give her the documents to allow her to get married, and even though she had a contract with RCA as a singer, she still could not get married without these documents.

The reason for them demanding her return, was that since she was now living in Italy, working hard and earning good money, as a singer, she had stopped sending them (the Socialist Party) all her money as they had demanded of her. She wanted nothing to do with her past life now and saw no reason to keep sending back all her hard-earned money to the Socialist Party in a country she no longer lived in.

The many letters were finding more and more reasons she should return to Prague. Working also through her mother, their demands were relentless now and became ever more threatening to get Yvonne back to Prague. But she still refused to go, knowing she would be jailed or even murdered once she set foot in her home country.

On Friday 18th of December, Yvonne called her mother to see how she was enjoying her visit to Prague and to ask her when my sister Simonne could spend some time with her there. Little did she know that was to be the last conversation she would ever have with her mother.

The following Monday the 21st. of December 1970, Yvonne's mother, my grandmother Magdalena Saghyova, was shot dead. She was murdered while in her home in Prague. Yvonne received a phone call from one of her mother's friends in Prague, the following day on the 22nd., saying her mother had been shot dead while in her own home that previous weekend.

There was nothing stolen from her home and no other motive other than the government's insistence to use her in order to get my mother Yvonne to return. There was no investigation to even try to find out who the killer was. Initially they tried to say her death was suicide, but later they changed that when it was widely known that my grandmother had never owned a gun and the wound was not in a place she could possibly have inflicted it herself, the back of her head.

She was a strong, much-loved woman and was well known to be a very stable person. Suicide was, therefore, completely out of the question. The fact they attempted to use this excuse proved her murder was being covered up.

The surgery, that she said prevented my sister from joining my grandmother, was very small, the removal of a small cyst, that would not have prevented my sister from traveling to Prague to be with her shortly after her procedure was completed to remove it.

We know now, on looking back, that perhaps she couldn't say anything over the phone as her mail and phone conversations were being monitored by the socialist authorities. Given their insistence that my mother should return, it was clear that she was using the very minor surgery as a reason to stop my mother from sending Simonne to be with her. In doing this, my grandmother had saved my sister's life.

My grandmother's murder was another way to get my mother to return there, if not as the result of their constant demands, then for her own mother's funeral when all other means had failed. Had my sister gone back to spend time with her grandmother what would have happened to her? Would she have been shot as well, because one thing is for certain, she would have been in the same house as her grandmother as a possible witness.

Would they hold Simonne as a child hostage in the same city Prague as they had with her mother, now using my sister as a new child hostage to get my mother to go back there?   After this tragic and vicious event, my mother realized all her misgivings and her subsequent decision not to return to that country under any excuse given, was what probably saved both hers and my sister's lives.

My grandparents' escape from Czechoslovakia was an embarrassment to the Czech socialist government. She was the one that got away. Nine years later, in 1979 and further on here in my book, I talk of a sudden fire that began in our apartment in Rome, when I was eight years old. It occurred shortly after a visit by my grandfather and his close friend, Jitka Frantova the famous actress and now ex-wife of the former Prague TV CEO, Jirí Pelikán, who was also, a close friend of the then Prime Minister, Alexander Dubcek who was also a close friend of my grandmother.

At the time of the Velvet Revolution, then going on in Czechoslovakia, in 1989 which led to the resignation of General Secretary, Milos Jakes, after an estimated 500,000 students and other people gathered to protest against the "One Party" socialist government there, things became very tense in Prague.

When Jiří Pelikán and Jitka Frantova escaped from Czechoslovakia, they took with them many, many, tape recordings, documents and other things that proved the high level of corruption going on within the socialist government, so they were both in a dangerous position.

Jirí Pelikán and Jitka Frantova, had to escape Czechoslovakia as soon as they saw a chance when the Velvet Revolution began and there was so much turmoil. My grandparents were in fact the very first family, in the entertainment industry, to leave Czechoslovakia.

Jiří Pelikán was married to my grandmother's close friend Jitka Frantova, who remained a still famous and very beautiful actress, Jiří Pelikán was, at the time, a political activist when they had both escaped to Italy following the demise of Czechoslovakia to the new socialist government.

Jitka Frantova, who came to visit with my father, remained a very well-known popular Czechoslovakian actress. On October 28th, 2015, at the Prague Castle, on the day of the National Holiday, she received, an Honor of "First Instance for the Services to the State in the Arts." from the hands of President Miloš Zeman, For her lifetime of work with the Czechoslovakian arts and film industry.

The murder of my grandmother in Prague, shortly after she returned there from Italy coupled with the intentionally set fire to our home in Rome, nine years later, after the visit of my grandfather and Jiří Pelikan's now, ex-wife Jitka Frantova, could not be considered a coincidence.

Following his visit to see us in Rome, the police were waiting for my grandfather, at the border, after he left our house to travel back to Prague. They completely stripped his car down to nothing but a heap of parts. They removed the seats, the tires from the wheels the upholstery and every single thing on my grandfather's car looking for something to arrest him for, leaving only a pile of parts where his car had once stood. How did they know his movements in advance? More of this later.

There was a growing list of terrible things happening to my family that only in hindsight we could connect the dots to see these were a sequence of targeted actions against my family.

Their refusal to join the socialist party, their success after a forced move into a completely nonrelated skill set to destroy them, the murder in Prague of my grandmother; the continuous string of increasingly more demanding letters insisting my mother return to

Prague and an arson attack on our family home. This was consistent bullying.

Many things can be seen as a coincidence but as time passes and with the benefit of hindsight, we often have more clarity to see things as they really were and coincidence becomes unlikely.

Chapter 8

Auschwitz Brought Home

Several years after we arrived in the U.S. My mother wanted to find out what had happened to her grandparents. She knew they had lived in Hungary and possibly in Czechoslovakia, but more than that she had no clue about their lives, how they lived or when they had died. Being Jewish was not something to talk about back then as Poland and other countries had become overrun by Nazi Germany. She had a forged passport (see photo) used to escape the Nazis in Hungary, but none of us knew more than that.

Even long after the war, no one ever talked about their history if they were Jewish and it was a taboo subject that people like my parents kept silent about long after World War II. They bore their memories and their scars, in silence just in case.

My mother knew there must have been a history and now she was determined to find out what it was from the safety of now living in America. She was never allowed to talk about her family and it was all kept quiet, which for a person like my mother was not going to be accepted forever. Being Jewish in Poland or Czechoslovakia was an extremely dangerous heritage to ever acknowledge being Jewish to anyone and was never discussed even within the family.

When we were living near Hollywood, my mother had a friend, who was President of the Jewish Community in Beverly Hills. She went to see him to see if he could help find out more about her grandparents and what may have happened to them back in Poland around the time of World War II. He suggested to her that she research her family history by contacting the Red Cross who had kept good records of all European countries affected by the Nazi regime including and especially those in Poland and Hungary.

So, she contacted the Red Cross, giving their names and all the information she had to help them identify where they were and to ask for their help in finding out what happened to them.

Three years later, the news finally reached us. The International Red Cross came back with some terrible news. Her grandfather, her grandmother and her uncle, had been shipped to Auschwitz, from Hungary where they were living and subsequently murdered by the Nazi's in their gas chambers in Auschwitz.

The information came as a complete shock which was made worse because The Red Cross had not only found the information about their names, but the document they sent showed on which train and in which railway carriage they traveled, in, to Auschwitz, from the Slovakian town of Banska Bystrica. They were obviously caught for being Jewish, which was reason enough to be sent to Auschwitz.

Added to this they had the time and date of their travel to the concentration camp at Auschwitz in that sinister train from Slovakia (see photo of their train ticket). They sent my mother the documents written in German showing all the information they had.

Typical of German efficiency, the document had dates and times of the train when it left and when it arrived. It was as if we were reading information about a **booking on a present**-day railway schedule with your carriage and seat number, taking the train to another city to go to the fair. But this was no fairground, this was something horrific and utterly evil.

Her grandparents' names were Daniel Grieser and Ilona Gabor and her mother's brother was Paul Grieser. The documents only showed details of her grandmother, but she knew they would probably have gone with her as they were very close.

I want to place their names here in my book for all who read my story to say their names out loud and to remember them, so their death will never be forgotten. This news was terrible for us all and we were all shocked into silence thinking about our family's past and what it meant for us all.

To get such terrible news like that, shook me to the core and it became not a story, about other people, told in grainy black and white images and told in jerky newsreels, stories of nameless strangers, or from old movies or articles written in some old-fashioned typeface, or in stories I may read about in history books, about the second world war.

Now it was my family who had been murdered along with millions of others and was part of my family's past and it was now part of my heritage. I cannot express my family's feelings about this, the horror, the sadness, the anger at their pointless death, we all felt on hearing the news. It left me speechless and so deeply sad that it seemed to have moved me to my very soul. I still think of them today and hope they are at peace now.

My mother found it especially hard to take in and went to see the Rabbi in Los Angeles to try to get some meaning in the news. My mother had visited Auschwitz, in 1961 with her mother, when she was traveling with the entertainment company, also in Krakow in Poland, but they had no idea that her own family had perished there and that maybe she was walking and seeing the very same death chamber her grandmother had been in. I don't want to go further down this rabbit hole but I want you my readers, to understand how this affected me and my family, it was real and words cannot express the deep feelings of sadness we all felt.

Even now writing this, it makes me stop and think back to how it must have been for all those people, human beings, family members, men, women and little innocent children, all traveling crammed into those trains, like cattle perhaps unknowing of the awful fate that awaited them all, to be exterminated by the Nazis in such an inhuman and horrific way. We must never forget these horrific events.

The horrific news brought the Holocaust, with all its horrors, right into our home, when we were now separated by a great distance, living in Hollywood.

My mother, following that news, spent many years trying to find out who her grandparents were, where they lived, anything at all about her grandparents' lives, but she could find out nothing at all. Sometimes we should leave our past where it belongs, in the past. I have included the documents the Red Cross gave us showing the train, the carriage and the date of departure and arrival of what to be my great grandparents last journey, the one they took to the Auschwitz death camp in Poland. Even now this makes me feel so sad for my family.

Rest in peace Daniel Grieser, Ilona Gabor and Paul Grieser, you will now live on forever here in my book.

Some things in a family's history are best left where they belong, back in the past, allowing us to move on so those in our past can be at peace.

Chapter 9

An Unforgettable Visit

I was born on February 29th, a leap year, in 1972 in Rome in the region of Lazio. My father and mother were both hard-working parents who brought my sister, Simonne and I up with strong beliefs that honesty, hard work, a good work ethic and to always arrive early would lead to our success.

My father was my hero, he was an accomplished, successful actor and entertainer in Italy born in Montelepre, Palermo on April 2, 1943, with a glittering career in movies.

Among my father's starring roles in films included *Grand Prix*, working with James Garner, Eva Marie Saint and Yves Montand. He was racing driver Nino Barlini. The film was directed by John Frankenheimer and won three Oscars.

The film also had other famous Formula 1 drivers, Bob Bondurant who raced for Shelby American, Ferrari, and Eagle teams. Jack Brabham Formula One World Champion in 1959, 1960, and 1966. Not credited were Jim Clark, who won two World Championships, in 1963 and 1965. He competed in the Indianapolis 500, which he won in 1965. Dan Gurney, who won races in the Formula One, Indy Car, NASCAR, Can-Am, and Trans-Am Series. Bruce McClaren who was a New Zealand racing car designer, driver, engineer and inventor. His name lives on in the McLaren team. Dad was in excellent company!

Grand Prix was shot on location during race weekends, with actors in real, moving cars (mostly F1 shells with F3 engines which were not quite as fast); action was filmed with in-car and mounted cameras, which didn't exist prior to the movie. In an article written by Priscilla Page she said, even 50 years on, the movie *Grand Prix* still put us on the edge of our seats. Way to go dad!

Among my father's many acting awards included being nominated for a Golden Globe award, in 1967, for "The Best Newcomer" that year, while we were still living in Italy.

He also starred in the, then famous, "Spaghetti Westerns" *One Dollar Too Many* and *Due Volte Giuda*. He carried on acting right until playing his role in, *The Bold and The Beautiful,* a TV series in 2006.

My parents met when my father went to a nightclub with a friend and my mother Yvonne was singing at the club. My father asked her to come over to join them, which she did for a short while, during her break, she then left their table. He called her back, saying, "Do you know who I am", while she was thinking, *do you know who I am?* Whenever she reminded me of those two phrases, I always smiled thinking of two strangers both thinking each was more famous than the other. Eventually they met for lunch and started dating.

At the time my father being a famous actor, was always driving a Ferrari, actually it was a convertible, one of many he bought directly from his friend Enzo Ferrari, which he drove around to help the image of Ferrari.

In fact, Enzo would often encourage my father to buy the latest model to drive and to be seen in, *made in Italy seen in Italy*. He drove cars like the 250 GTS, which now would be worth over a million dollars, but then in the early sixties, it was worth less than ten thousand! Time seems to re-value everything.

When I was only eight years old and my sister was ten, my mother took the family to see the concentration camp, Terezin, just outside Prague in Czechoslovakia, where we could see first-hand what the horror of Nazi Germany was really about.

When we arrived there, we could feel the evil that hung in the air and it was very real. We saw the buildings and the hundreds of photos that were so horrific to us and we found it all so terrible to see. But to see it was to remember those who were murdered and we should never ever forget the face of evil. At eight years old I was horrified at seeing what had been done to the Jews and I will never forget what I saw there for as long as I live.

Terezin left an indelible impression on both my sister and me. It was something we can never ever forget and neither will we ever want to, as our small tribute to all those people who died there.

When we were leaving Czechoslovakia, after that unforgettable visit, to get back to Italy, we had to pass through border customs. The customs officers, upon seeing our belongings, took all my toys; my inflatable toy canoe, everything they could find. Calmly they climbed into our car, making us stand around outside, as we watched them steal everything.

I asked my mother, "Why did they do that, why did they take my canoe?" She simply said, "Because they can." I couldn't understand those words. They took our books, our personal belongings and all my toys. They matter-of-factly stole everything we had! As I was to find out later in my life, some people do unlawful things, "because they can!"

To learn first-hand at that age, when I was eight years old, what communism and socialism was all about left a lasting impression that

I will never forget and neither I nor my family would ever want to be part of communism or socialism ever.

As my own family experienced first-hand, socialism has never worked in any countries where my family lived and there is no country where it has ever gone well for the working people. It promises equality for all and delivers this but not as one would imagine. It delivers misery for all and no one has any control over their lives.

If we cannot change a bad situation, we can try to move on from it.

Chapter 10

A Career Slowing Down

However good my father's very successful movie career was in Italy, with 60 films to his credit. However, the work begun to slow down. The reason was the continual stream of Hollywood movies hitting the world stage. They had the benefit of instant subtitles and voice dubbing. We were seeing the beginning of a nationwide slowdown in all businesses right across Italy, which of course included and especially the Italian film industry.

There are many opinions as to why Italy, the country of Ferrari, fine wines and superb world-renowned fashion, was declining. But we saw it for what it was, a country going down because of a never-ending series of bad political decisions and a move further over into socialism. This meant we had to consider moving for my father to get more work, make money and to be seen by a much bigger audience, at least that was what we hoped.

We had numerous friends and family members in Italy so to consider moving away was a major and life-changing decision, but with his work slowing down to a stand-still and with a young family to feed, it was either that or go into a completely new career. To start a new career, my father would have had to leave his lifetime of work in films. Leaving all that behind to do something else was out of the question, especially in a country slowly going downhill.

My mother was also a real hero in my eyes, then and now. Many times, when we were struggling to make ends meet, having little money for food, she would make some inexpensive soup and take that to work making it her only meal of the entire day. She learned that from her mother. Yes, things were that tough with so little money coming in.

My mom and dad never discussed, with me or my sister, how bad things were for the family, when my father's acting was becoming so difficult with no more work anywhere. They never wanted us to be aware of the problems they both faced.

But, when it came time for a big decision, it was short, "this is what we will do, this is how it is and this is what you need to understand." There were never big family discussions, so my sister and I were, for the most part, protected from the reality that was now all around us. We were going broke though and without money everything stops!

Moving on is sometimes a decision that is already made for us by circumstances beyond our control.

Chapter 11

Escape

While under pressure from the Czechoslovakian socialist Party, President Edvard Benes allowed a socialist-dominated government to be organized in Czechoslovakia. It was virtually a bloodless socialist coup and it was an example of Soviet expansion into Eastern Europe. When my grandmother escaped, from Czechoslovakia to Hungary, it was because it was a dangerous place for a Jewish person to live in the 1940's. She escaped with forged passports and documents (see photo).

Before the second world war, Czechoslovakia was a democratic country, a beautiful place to live and people were happy there. Following the single party system set up by the socialist leadership it became dismal and people were unhappy. Then in 1989, there was a revolution, called The "Velvet Revolution," and before that Czechoslovakia was a Socialist Republic (CSSR) ruled then, by a party system based the communist party. The country belonged to the Eastern Bloc and was a member of the Warsaw Pact and Comecon.

I want to explain all this as it is part of my family's background and explains how we see the pitfalls of socialism ruining a once thriving country. During the era of Communist controlled socialist party rule, thousands of Czechoslovakians faced political persecution for various drummed up offences and for such things as trying to emigrate across the Iron Curtain. This was strange to me to have to fight to keep people within the country who wanted to leave because they didn't have the freedom to be able to live there.

They saw life in Czechoslovakia getting steadily worse and ordinary things, food, clothing, and all normal things we need to survive were getting harder and harder to find, even if the family had work and had an income. This was the ugly face of socialism and I can tell you from all that my family went through, socialism from our experience didn't work.

My father had also to deal with tragedy and loss, himself, when his father died in his arms. My father was only 16 years old at the time and was living in Sicily. After this he had no money at all, as his brothers all went their separate ways leaving him to fend for himself as a teenager after his father's death.

Before that, my dad had a big and seemingly very close family when they all lived in Palermo in Sicily, (see photo) but after his father died, our once huge family, all disappeared and my father's side of his family split up. All his brothers, my uncles, went their own separate ways, so he had no help to get through his own father's death and at only 16 years of age. There would have been five brothers, uncles to me, but the last one died at birth. All that was left was my aunt Dilva and my dad.

When his mother died all his brothers were arguing at her funeral over what they each wanted from her belongings. One brother, in particular, was Santo, dad's oldest brother, who was really making demands as if her belongings belonged to him, not caring for her memory and all she had done for them. My dad was disgusted with them all.

The fact was, it was my father who had bought her everything she owned, so this was one time when my father got furious with them and told them all to get out and go away and he was dead serious! My father never looked back and didn't care if he ever saw them again because it wasn't about their mother's possessions it was the fact that she had died and they had not shown her any respect.

This was what split them all up and my father's family never got back together. It was a shame and my father told me that after the death of his mother, the family all went their own separate ways, perhaps for the better.

Despite all the troubles and the lack of money my father and mother were experiencing, while the movie industry was slowing down, they never said anything to Simonne and me. We were unaware of their problems with having little to no money as they never discussed these things in front of us. My mother kept working as many jobs as she could and never showed my sister and I the stress they were both under.

I can't imagine how sad my father must have been seeing his life's work, as a successful actor, well known throughout Italy, gradually grinding to a halt, but he never showed us his feelings. Strange how his life is so similar to my life now, no work in the industry we both love. But as for our family, we remained close and we decided we would move on to better things.

A close family can overcome anything.

Chapter 12

Losing Everything

Our home was located at the starting point of an ancient Roman road leading from Rome and heading to the Northwest of Italy. From the windows of our home, we could see across a big valley with pine trees and we had farmland around us, with no buildings in view, which was rare in Rome. The "Tomba di Neros," (Nero's Tomb) was just down the street from our home. He was the emperor who allegedly fiddled while Rome burned.

One day, in June 1979, when I was seven years old, I was at home watching our dog Rudy, a Yorkie, who eventually lived to be 17 years old. Rudy came with our family from Italy to America, then back to Italy with us and again back to the America, more of this later. On this day, however, I was in our kitchen when Rudy suddenly ran into the kitchen barking loudly. He had never ever behaved like that, so I followed him into the living room to see what was wrong.

As I followed him I could smell something burning and it was getting stronger. I rushed into the living room, to see a fire had started behind the TV. I thought it seemed to have been caused by something at the back of the TV, but it came out of nowhere and was burning very fast with flames shooting upwards. Suddenly the curtains caught alight with a whoosh right behind the TV. How the fire started from nothing at all, was hard to understand especially as there had never been any problems with our TV or any other electrical things in our home. The curtains caught fire and very quickly the flames shot up to the ceiling with smoke everywhere. It seemed only seconds before the flames spread along the ceiling and across the room.

I was terrified, but I was also mesmerized, watching the flames quickly spreading across the room right before my eyes. The flames were becoming so hot and spreading fast across the ceiling above me when I knew I had to do something or just get out fast.

In our living room we had many fine antiques, beautiful furniture, original oil paintings from famous artists, that my parents had collected over many years. I didn't know what to do, as I stood in the room that was rapidly becoming engulfed in flame. I grabbed a hose that we used in the garden, but realized I couldn't use it because now the fire was everywhere and far too powerful for a small garden hose to make any difference.

I tried to throw water on it, but nothing could stop the flames from spreading and I was scared for me and for Rudy. We had so much in that room personal things that seemed to spontaneously burst into flames immediately catching fire. Very soon the room was engulfed in flames, seemingly in only seconds and I was really scared now. I had never seen a fire like this before and I couldn't believe how fast it was spreading right in front of me.

I wanted to open the shutters to get out but the chords had burned through so I couldn't. I was becoming trapped and ran to the back of the house and, grabbing Rudy, I ran out as quickly as I could. I ran down the stairs, holding him in my arms. Just as I reached the ground floor I went outside; I looked up and saw a wall of bright orange flames behind the windows. Suddenly there was a loud explosion, as all the windows upstairs exploded out onto the street where I was standing. Glass was falling all around me; it was a miracle that I wasn't cut to pieces.

Someone had called the fire department and I could hear their sirens getting louder as they approached our home. There were so many fire trucks with lights and sirens on, the firefighters immediately started to rush around laying hoses and running towards our home. Now the entire upper part of the building was ablaze with bright orange flames shooting out of what were once our windows.

I was scared and wanted to find my father before he got to our burning home, I didn't know what to do so I started running down our street to a junction at the corner, in the direction where I knew my mom and dad would come from, as they always did. I stood there on that corner ready to wave them down so they could see me before they got to the fire.

Of course, there were no cell phones and no social media so there was no way to call or reach my parents, all I could do was watch and wait for them. In the meantime, while I was waiting on the corner, my dad had arrived, but from the opposite direction and he didn't see me. It was like a movie, both hoping to meet but in different locations. Dad immediately went to run into the house, but the firefighters were trying to stop him. He was screaming out my name at the top of his lungs, thinking I was still in the house.

They were not going to stop him and he was getting inside the house regardless of how hard they tried. My dad pushed them out of the way and ran into the burning building shouting my name as loud as he could.

He broke through their line and kicked our very sturdy solid wood front door open. To this day we have no idea how he managed that as the front door was made with extremely thick wood and was rock solid. But he had superhuman strength at that moment and broke in. He ran into all the rooms he could, looking for me not knowing I was not there.

It's hard to imagine what he was thinking, how terrified he was, believing I was still inside our now fully involved burning home. He even ran upstairs, ignoring the heat, to see if I was there, but the flames and smoke were getting worse by the second and held him back. By now, my dad was franticly looking for me and shouting out my name. He thought I was gone!

Meanwhile, back outside on the street there was a crowd gathering including some boys on motorbikes watching all that was going on. My dad went over to them, to tell them, not asking but telling them, to please go look and for me all around our neighborhood, in all directions, as they all knew me.

I was still sitting on the corner waiting with Rudy, when I saw two kids on motorbikes racing towards me. One of them said, "Are you Antonio?" I said yes, though I didn't recognize them. He said, "Your dad had sent us and some others out to find you!"

I jumped on his motorbike behind him, holding Rudy on my lap as we raced back to my house riding as fast as we could go all the way up the hill.

By the time we arrived, firemen were everywhere and there were now fifteen or more fire trucks all parked outside, with ladders up and water being poured into our home. But the flames were so high now and the entire house was fully consumed, engulfed in flames! The house was like an oven, everything was being consumed by the flames, we had antiques, gold cannons, silver medallions, paintings, and everything was being melted to the ground.

What was strange was, as I was to find out later, our gold ornaments, had all apparently melted but, as we were to learn later, the temperature of the heat in the fire could not have been hot enough to melt the gold and silver, but we were told this is what had happened to our most treasured possessions. More likely they had been stolen.

My dad was still waiting at the top of the hill where our house was located and I was coming towards him on the back of a motocross bike. As we approached, I could see him standing there in tears, thinking I was gone. I jumped off the still moving motorbike as I got close to him and he grabbed me with a great big bear hug.

That was the first time I ever saw my dad, a big, strong, larger-than-life papa, in tears crying and sobbing while he held me tightly. His tears were not for the house and all we had lost was because I was alive.

While this was going on my mom was with my sister Simonne, at a piano recital some distance away, at **Palazzo Barberini** when two policemen came running up to her, told her about the fire and asked her how many children she had. Immediately she was very concerned and wanted to know why they had asked her this.

When she told them she had two children, but Simonne was with her. They told her everyone was accounted for, but now she was in desperate need of information. She called the house but of course there was no answer. So, she left immediately and drove home as fast as she could in her Mini Cooper, which went like a bat out of hell!

Our home was at the top of a hill and as she approached, she could usually see it from over a mile away, but because of the heavy pall of smoke surrounding what was our home and the fact that it was now becoming dark, the flames were dying down. Now all that she saw as she drove closer was the dark remains of our home, there were no lights and there were at lease fifteen fire trucks and almost as many police cars and ambulances surrounding our home.

She couldn't get close because all the traffic was now at a standstill on the approach to our home, so Simonne was hanging out the car window screaming for the cars to let them through. They left their car on the side of the road and started to run towards what was our home but was now a smoldering mass of smoking rubble where the fire had consumed everything.

As she approached, by foot, both Rome's fire chief and the city police chief came up to her and told her all were accounted for adding that Antonio Sr. and Antonio Jr. were at the police station for their safety. It was then that they told my mother it was a bomb that had caused the fire and it had gone off while I was alone in our house.

Simonne told me later that all she could see as they were approaching our home was a huge pall of black smoke and the structure had almost completely gone. The four of us just stood on the street, staring in sad, shocked silence at, what was only a couple of hours before, our beautiful home with all we had ever owned inside.

We could do nothing as we had nowhere to go and nothing to take with us. All our clothes, all our belongings, everything we had once owned was now gone. We were stranded, right there on our own street, looking into an abyss that was our home, surrounded by strangers, slowly leaving us to deal with this utter devastation that was once our home. We stood in silence for a long time as the meaning of what we were looking at slowly sank in.

There were no words we could say to each other that might have explained the meaning of this to any of us, standing there staring in stunned silence. Why this had happened and who had done this was for later but not now.

As I was to find out many, many years later, the fire chief, at the scene, told my parents it was an incendiary bomb that had caused the fire and the following day, on the 1st of June, this revelation was headlines in all the papers at the time but I never read the newspapers, so I didn't know it then.

Mom and dad kept it from my sister me, so we wouldn't worry. Why or who would do this doesn't matter now but I was lucky to have escaped with my life, with the speed that the fire had spread.

Part of our healing after a disaster, is picking ourselves up and starting again.

Chapter 13

Life in Italy

There were many buildings and many children in the gated community, of Via Cassia, where we lived, in Rome, Italy. Many remain my close friends even today since we were six years old. Some even to this day still live there in Via Cassia. I had my family and my cousins around and we had such a great time there and I loved it.

As a child I never spent much time inside as I was always out on the streets, where I preferred to be, playing with my friends. But because of my father's work, in a lifetime of making movies and my mother's hard work, we could afford to live in one of the best areas in Rome.

I was always the one, out of all my friends, who "crossed the bridge" that's to say I was the one who tried anything first, took on the "dare" before any of my friends would dare to do something.

I was the leader, the only one to go outside of our community and into the valley or down to the stream that was also there in the valley. We built tree houses and forts there and had such a great time every day. I took my "boys" with me, Corrado, Umberto, Giancarlo and Giulio and Giulio's brother Mario. We were a team and did everything together.

There was a landscaper living in our community who had a little house (an elaborate shed) for all his tools and lawn mowers that he kept locked up inside. But right above the locked door, there was a small round hole in the wall. It was a tight-fit, but I got in through that hole. I did it by climbing up a tree outside his tiny house and shinnying along a branch until I reached that hole in the wall where I climbed in and opened the door from the inside, to get the tools I needed to build our tree house.

After school, we always had homework to do, but I rushed through mine and it was me who always called on the others to come and play. Some kids took a nap after school, while others stayed at home but not us, we had way too much to do. We had our secret place and we made sure no one knew about it.

When my father was busy making movies, he never took Simonne and I to see him on the film set and at the time we were too busy to care. But despite the slowdown, my father and mother saved up all they could and bought a small boat in need of much repair.

My dad used his strength and ability to rebuild it for the family to use in summer. When he had finished the boat looked great and we were happy to be in it all through our summer holidays. One thing of the things I admired about my dad was that he always made time to keep himself fit and it was a priority for him despite the demanding schedule of his acting. This he passed on to me becoming a priority in my career also.

We took our boat to the coast and stayed on that boat all summer long. It was inexpensive for us to do this but that didn't seem to matter. We sailed it down the coast and back. We loved our life on the ocean. We stayed for the whole month of August living on our boat and these were happy times for us all.

One time the local kids thought they could pick on me as the son of a famous actor. But when they did pick on me, I would give it right back. I knew I could never take them all at once because they were much bigger than me. One time, however, after a particularly aggressive pushing and pulling me around while making threats to me, when I was much smaller and younger than they were, I told my dad about one of the boys who lived downstairs and who had always been picking on me.

My dad went to their apartment downstairs and knocked on their door asking them to come outside. He asked the boy to come outside to talk to him and I remember my dad saying through the door, "I want to talk about what you are doing with my boy!" The boy wouldn't come out, but that stopped him from ever bullying me again. My hero, my dad!

Dad would never put up with bullies and was afraid of no one. Having grown up and seeing my dad lose it with someone, I know how easily I could have grown up to be the same, but I didn't. In my father's defense he only wanted to be respected that's all and would never let anyone talk down to him or insult him. He had five brothers and four sisters growing up, so he learned to stand up for himself.

Not giving into bullies is a trait both my father and I shared.

Chapter 14

A Decision by Fire

After the fire, for my sister and I, it was the absolute loss of all we had ever known, all that we had in our world and that was a very scary time for us both. We were all facing a very uncertain future, we were at a loss, not knowing what our parents would do now or what was in store for our future. We went as a family to spend that summer on our boat, away from Rome and what had been the terrible incident of the fire. How it was deliberately how it started as an arson attack, why and by whom were questions left unanswered.

After this terrible fire, none of our so called "friends" who had all been around us, while my father's career had been at its crest, lifted a finger to help us. They had been to our home, enjoyed our generous hospitality, my family's undemanding and honest friendship. They were people who we thought, good friends who enjoyed rubbing shoulders with my famous parents and who we thought were our close friends. We were wrong.

Not one of them bothered to lift a finger to help us get back on our feet. We were shocked at how shallow they all were, but we were to find out that this was, sadly, quite normal for people who become "friends" in the movie industry. I learned this lesson at eight years old, that just because people smile and seem to be close, many are not and as soon as times get tough, they all melt away, never offering help. We loved our home in the ancient city of Rome, our life and all we had ever known was there. We knew the streets, the shops, the shopkeepers, even the unique and familiar smell of our hometown in Rome. We were an indelible part of life there. I had known no other life other than my life in Rome with all it held for me and my family.

Work for my father after the fire had remained all but non-existent and things were quite tough for us. But our living needs were not in any way excessive even when my father's career in movies was going very well. We were used to only having what we needed as my parents had always been careful with money. My mother was still working in a boutique so at least we had an income.

A decision to move.

We made the decision, following that fire, that we would emigrate to America. We talked about moving to Hollywood, the center of the movie industry, so my father could hopefully pick up his career there.

Part of me was excited at the opportunity of a new life in the States, as I had seen some of what America was like from TV shows and movies, it was intriguing to me. But another part of me was fearful of what our new life, in a new country would be like, knowing almost no one and worse still we only spoke Italian.

We loved all we had seen and learned about America so that part of the decision was easy, but nevertheless the move, from Italy to the U.S.A. was to be life-changing for us all. We had always done everything as a family and we would make the decision and the move as a family. I knew at a very young age, maybe because of my father's acting and our life with the Italian film industry, that I loved everything I heard saw or read about life in America and the movie industry there.

We never learned English at school as we had no reason to do so. My father's work was mainly in the Italian movie industry, making movies for the Italian movie market. He had been in movies that were not for an English-speaking audience, he could at least speak a little English but certainly not enough to get by. As for my sister Simonne and I however, English was never required and never taught.

A new life in another country half the world away was an exciting but daunting feeling for us all. For my parents, a new job and for my sister and I, a new school, new friends and a new city was also overwhelming, but we also trusted our parents and we both knew they would do what was right for us all.

Since my father was in the movie industry, I had grown up, occasionally watching them, seeing them being made and with the many conversations with my father, I understood all that went into making a movie. I was fascinated by what I saw coming out of Hollywood and was amazed at the differences in style, in the subject matter of the world-famous movies and especially with their special effects. Compared with the Italian movies being made, Hollywood movies were, for me, much more exciting.

I was in love with the movie industry and with Hollywood before I was eight years old. I spent many hours watching movies, imagining that I was in the film as an actor.

I had been captivated at a young age by all I had seen and imagined even as a boy, that one day I would be in one of these movies. I often thought about what it would be like to become a part of the "movie magic." Despite this, I knew there was also the downside as I have mentioned, leaving my school friends who I had known all my life, our relatives and our family friends.

Thoughts about our decision to move were in my mind constantly, but it was also exciting to think of living in the States. This would be an interesting time for us and a bittersweet time for us all. I had never had to say goodbye to anyone, but now I would do it with everyone I ever knew.

So, the decision was made, we were moving to America and we were going to live in Hollywood, California close to the movie industry, to begin our lives again. This was now summer 1985; I was twelve-years old. We were now hoping to join the millions of immigrants who had made America what it is today.

Once the decision was made there were so many things to get done. A silent thought for each of us still lingered in our minds, that fire was a deliberate act and if we remained in Rome what would come next? Moving out of Rome and out of Italy was the only decision, and as a family, would make it work no matter what.

Once a decision is made, do it and don't second guess.

Chapter 15

Doing It Right

It was not easy at all going through the process as an immigrant family wanting to come to America legally. It took my parents five long years to complete the process and that was not to mention the money we had to pay. It cost my family many thousands of dollars to pay for the process and this was when there was little to no film work for my father. We had to have x-rays, medical exams, bloodwork and so many interviews. Some interviews were at a moment's notice, so we had to drop everything to go to the American Embassy in Rome, to do whatever they wanted us to do. The process was onerous to say the least and it was as if the US didn't want us there, but we were determined to emigrate.

The entire process took more money than we had ever saved and although my mother had her boutique, every penny she made was going to our application to get to America. With what I see now, thirty years on from those days, the illegal immigrants coming up from or through Mexico do not have to meet or go through these stringent conditions and in fact they are given housing, free medical coverage and even money to live on. We were given none of these things arriving legally, from a friendly country, despite having paid many thousands of dollars to eventually get here legally.

But for us, we knew that anything worthwhile is never easy to obtain and the harder it was the more determined we were to make it. I had been brought up to believe that nothing is free everything has to be earned. This lesson was taught to my sister Simonne and I; it was a life lesson that both my father and mother taught us our whole life. We knew that we had done all that was required of us, we had to hope and pray that all would be okay for us to proceed with our green card applications.

Waiting in line was all we could do now and we heard nothing for months after our last interview. We had no idea what the background checks were all about and even if these would be acceptable for the U.S. Immigration authorities. Although I was young, I knew this was it, this was what we wanted, to live in the U.S. and no matter what, we had to make it into America.

One day, completely out of the blue, the process we began five years earlier, finally came to fruition. We received a phone call from the U.S. Embassy in Naples, asking us to come immediately for an interview, it was 5am and we were told almost nothing before we went, except that we had an opportunity and had to go there and not be late for our upcoming appointment!

We were all excited and a little nervous as we left home immediately to get to the U.S. Embassy, but we were also determined to leave Italy for America, so this was part of the process. We had no idea whether we had successfully filled out all the information required or even if there was a space for us to make it in, but we were told this was an opportunity.

We felt blessed that our time had finally come, after a 5-year process and hopefully this was an entrance interview. When we arrived in Naples, we were told we had to collect everything together. We had to get photos done, not just snapshots, but photos requiring that we all went to a professional photographer who knew what was required. We managed to get together all the legal documents, our application documents and to make sure we left nothing behind. We did it, we gathered all we had been asked to take with us and we were ready to go.

The embassy we were to go to was in the city of Naples, to the south of Rome. Our drive there would take us considerable time and we were to be there at 6 am. Knowing we now had another, hopefully final, interview, along with a chance to emigrate to America, was exciting, we were now eager to see what our chances were.

The interview went well, reviewing our papers, going over our application, we were asked to assure the immigration authorities we would not be using social security, nor were we involved in any political parties and we would earn our own way and not become a burden on the American taxpayer. Then finally we were told we had been accepted!

We were walking on air when we knew we had finally made it through the last interview and through the long and costly immigration process, now we could focus on leaving Italy to begin a new life all over again.

In order for us to move, my mother had to take care of everything in Rome, she rented out our home, selling what things she could while setting up bank accounts for us to access money once we were in America. It was her hard work that enabled us to survive once we landed in America.

Anything that is hard to achieve makes it even more valuable when we finally achieve it!

Chapter 16

The Land of the Free

It was now summer 1985, after saying our sad, but fond goodbyes to all our friends and family, my father and I left for America ahead of my mother and sister so we could get everything set up before they arrived. We both stayed near Hollywood in a motel room that we both shared. My dad and I began the search for somewhere more permanent to live before bringing my mom and my sister over.

Around a month later when my mom and sister finally arrived. My family was back together again at last. But now we were in Hollywood. I couldn't believe we were all finally here. The apartment we could afford was not in the best part of Hollywood, but we didn't care, we were where we wanted to be and after what had happened to our home in Rome, we were in Hollywood, USA!

When we arrived in California, we had no credit and no ability to rent an apartment except paying in cash. We got no help from the authorities and were left to fend for ourselves, but we found a place to live. My mother had rented out our home in Italy and that money helped us over this financial hurdle.

We didn't speak any English and had to learn it quickly. We soon found a local school for my sister Simonne and me. We found it difficult at first in our new school as the other kids spoke so fast and our ears were not yet used to the English language.

It took around four months for me to learn the basics of English, I did it mostly by watching American movies. I took the bus from our apartment and went to the movie theater as many times as I could, where I sat and repeated lines over and over to myself.

My favorite film was *Top Gun* and I watched that film over and over again, learning almost line-by-line every word spoken by Tom Cruise. Little did I know that I would eventually meet him in person, but that's for later on.

I didn't want to have an accent when I spoke. I had to learn exactly how each word was pronounced, I wanted very much to sound like a local and to learn how people sounded so I mimicked each word to get that sound in my voice. Thank you, Tom Cruise, for teaching me a new language! I learned everything about speaking English from listening to you.

I also went to as many speech lessons as I could and I practiced at home in front of the mirror, with my sister, so we were both trying out our new language skills with each other. It took time, around four months, but gradually over time our English became easier and I found could speak English with little to no accent.

My mother worked three jobs to make ends meet so we could move to Hollywood. My father was prepared to do anything and that included him working for a builder's merchant, selling building materials which he was not used to, but we loved it all and we were determined to make it as a family, but most of all, we were fine with everything.

I have to say here that I held both my parents in such high esteem for the way they both just got on with making this work. My dad especially after being a famous actor in Italy to now working at any job, no matter how humble and to never complain, but to just do what it took to help us live the American Dream. My mom was a singer, actress, dancer, but here she was also working in shops doing whatever she could. Many times, she had three jobs at the same time. I love my mom and dad more than words could ever express. We made it through those tough times as a close family, but the burden was on our mom and dad to keep a roof over our head and to provide money for rent and food.

I learned a lot going through this, mainly because I would need this drive to succeed later on in my life. It seemed, looking back, that I was being prepared for what was to come and we only see and understand this when we look back at all that has happened with the knowledge of what we are facing later in life.

Parents often never know what the little things they do, become the things that leave an indelible impression on us as children.

Chapter 17

<hr>

Hands in The Cookie Jar

<hr>

It was when I was at Hawthorne School, at thirteen years old, that I seemed to be always hungry, especially after school. I knew that there was always food in one of the upstairs classrooms. One day I had the urge to get back into the school building, after classes had finished to get some cookies that I knew were in that room.

There was a very large tree just outside the school, right next to the school building and I knew I could climb that big tree, noticing that there was a window on the second floor that, I hoped, I could open if I reached out from one of the big tree branches after I climbed up.

I looked around, the street was empty, or so I thought. With one last look around me, I began to climb the tree. Up I went, branch by branch, like a monkey, until I had reached the height of the second-floor window. I carefully inched my way along a big branch until I was close to the window. I reached over and pushed on the window and to my surprise it wasn't locked. So, after taking another look around, I climbed into the classroom.

I carefully climbed off the branch into the classroom and began to search for the cookies that I knew were inside. The blinds were all down as they often were because of the bright sunlight which, during the day and particularly in the early evening, was far too bright. This made the room I was in quite dim.

I found the tin full of cookies, in one of the teacher's desk drawers, then sat down on the teacher's chair with my feet on his desk to eat them feeling thrilled with myself. Funny thing, most kids can't wait to get out of school and here was me breaking into school, but that was me, always doing the opposite. All was silent except for the sound of my munching, echoing around the completely empty classroom.

Anyway, all was fine until, the door suddenly opened and in stepped a police officer with his long flashlight pointing right in my face! I froze with a cookie in my mouth and one in my hand, poised to place the next one in my mouth. "What are you doing in here!" the officer said in a very stern authoritative voice, while noticing all the crumbs on the teacher's desk.

I tried to hide the cookie in my hand by hiding it behind my back, but for that beady eyed cop, it was too late, I was caught red-handed and as they say, "with my hand in the cookie jar," someone had ratted me out!

I could think of nothing to say, so I told the truth, "I just came in to get some cookies," I said. "Well, you're not supposed to be here and you were seen climbing that tree outside," he said as he walked over to the window to look outside to see the tree I had climbed up.

He closed the window and made sure it was locked, turning back to me he said, "you're coming with me son" he said as he came over and grabbed my arm to take me with him. "Where are you taking me?" I asked him, "to the police station," he told me. I was now a little scared of what that may entail but I kept quiet as I didn't want to make it worse.

Off we went, me and the cop, down the stairs of the completely empty school building, that was usually very noisy and full of students and teachers. Now all we could hear was the sound of our footsteps walking along the corridors and stairs. We went outside to where the police cruiser was waiting with its two-tone lights blazing for the whole world to see. I wished those glaring lights were switched off so we could go quietly and no one could see me but that was not to be, they were on as bright as can be, just for me.

We drove to the police station where I was questioned as to how I managed to break into the school and I told them of my excellent tree climbing abilities, they were not impressed however and told me they were calling my parents. I tried to tell them that the window was already open, so I didn't break in, I just climbed in. But they were not listening and instead they called my dad.

My dad arrived to pick me up trying to look stern, but not really managing it. Luckily for me there were no charges, but what charges could they have leveled at me? *Your honor, he stole 4 cookies!* But I was in trouble at school and was now somewhat famous as the boy who broke into the school to steal cookies.

My mom, though, was furious with me and told me off; making me promise never to attempt that again. "It's not like you are starved!" my mother told me, "We feed you plenty of food and you certainly don't look half starved, so why did you do it?" she asked me. I told her I just wanted to see if I could climb that tree and I knew there were always cookies in that classroom. She gave me her stern look, that could freeze hot water, then the matter was over.

I had to replace the ones I had eaten but it could have been far worse for me if they had expelled me from the school. I felt extremely lucky and also a little stupid too and promised my parents, the police and the school, that I would never do anything like this again.

There are decisions, actions we take from our decisions and then the consequences of our actions as I had just found out!

Chapter 18

Plans Interrupted

We couldn't make ends meet despite my mother working several jobs, we still had no money, which was heartbreaking for my parents, especially for my father who tried everything to find work. As a result, our American dream was not to be and we had to move back to Italy. But it was decided that my sister, Simonne, should stay behind as she was at a critical time with her schooling.

She became an au pair, to a doctor and his family, who lived opposite the school, earning her keep and living with them, while dad, mom and I were all back in Italy. This was very difficult for her being separated from our family, but she managed it, as she had to back then, there was no other choice.

Once again, my father my mother and I had to leave our home, now in the U.S. and we had to move back to Italy to stay in our home, which up to that time had been rented out. Things had not worked out as planned and we were not doing well in the U.S.

When we arrived back in Italy my father worked in a car dealership with my aunt, so that we had some money coming in at last. My parents insisted that I should be placed in dental school of all things, as my parents told me, "Antonio, being a dentist is a great career and you will have a very well-paid job for life!" I hated it and certainly never saw myself as a budding dentist. Me, a dentist! Looking back, I know they were right and I could have had a great and steady career as a dentist, but no way was that for me. Life is more than a steady income from something I knew I would hate doing.

We stayed in Italy, this second time, for seven months before my father decided we needed to be back in the USA. This stage of my life became difficult as my heart was now in America and I was dying to get back there. I felt I didn't fit in anymore in Italy. My schooling, my friends, the way of life, everything was now different for me and I realized I didn't belong there.

We knew we had to get back to America so my mother, once again, arranged everything to do with the selling of our home in Rome, Italy, to enable us to buy another home in Hollywood, following our return to America.

This time we moved to Marina del Rey and I went to a Catholic school, St. Bernard's, at Playa del Ray. I hated wearing school uniforms and conforming to a life that the school forced onto me. I didn't like this at all. The education though was excellent, but I was a rebel. I got into several fights and got sent home from school more than once. I then began hanging out with the football team while I was there wanting to become part of the team and to be accepted as a local boy rather than an immigrant.

The education and the teachers there were good, but it was not for me. I was then placed in Venice High School, where they filmed Grease with John Travolta and Olivia Newton John. The constant moving around made it difficult for any continuity with my education. I had to do my sophomore year twice. I left high school early in my junior year and I did not make it through to graduation. It was because I was so far behind the other kids; not only from changing schools, but switching between countries, which resulted in my hatred of school.

I had to do something to change my situation. I wanted to drop out of school because I was so far behind. My dad would never ever accept me drifting around with nothing to do so I had to think about what it was I wanted out of life and I had to make it happen by myself and for myself. One thing for certain, no one was going to do it for me.

To say these were difficult times, for all of us, would be an understatement. We had no help, as other illegal immigrants have today, no free money, no free health and no accommodation other than what we found and provided for ourselves.

But we knew this when we arrived here and, as a close family, we knew we would make it no matter what. But I want to explain that knowing this did not make it any easier for us. Looking back, it was coming through those times that prepared me for what was to come later in my own life.

Plans interrupted are not necessarily plans finished.

Chapter 19

My Schools

I went to several schools, one of which was Beverly Hills High, after we had first moved to California. It was on Moreno Drive, Beverly Hills in California. The school was a modern building with four floors, built in light gray stone with green tinted windows. Everything was exactly as I had seen it in the many movies, I had avidly watched, when we were back in Italy showing US schools. The school was quite different to what I had been used to. Whereas my school in Rome was an old building, in a residential part of Rome, this one was very modern and very well equipped. There were hallways with lockers in this school and I had my own locker. Lockers were never present at my school in Italy, probably because of a lack of space.

Beverly Hills Junior High and the High School were both among the most highly rated schools around, with over eighteen hundred students and with only eighteen students to each teacher. It was also the "school for the stars" where actors like Richard Dreyfus, Nicolas Cage, David Schwimmer, Tori Spelling, Lenny Kravitz, and the world-famous Andre Previn all of whom had attended this school. This made it a highly desirable place for me to be. My mom and dad wanted my sister and I to have the absolute best start here and this was part of their plan. They had thought of everything.

Again, having no credit, we had trouble renting an apartment, but my dad knew the manager of a building, which was perfect for us, and we decided to live there. My mother had saved all her money earned in Rome and had rented our home there, to make enough money to get us established in America and to cover our costs after we arrived.

If it were not for her scrimping and saving and then renting out our home in Rome, we couldn't have begun to make it here in America, back then there was no assistance for immigrants, and we were *legal* immigrants.

Where we lived during that time was in Hollywood, but earlier when I was attending Beverly Hills Junior High we did not live in Hollywood and although it wasn't a bad area at all, it was just one that I didn't want others at school to know about in case they saw me as an outsider or coming from a different lower-class side of town. I have to say though that the school was so elitist that they even sent snoops to check out where their students lived and if you weren't living in Beverly Hills, they wouldn't accept you at the school, so we kept our residence a secret.

Best of all were the sports facilities and we had amazing football grounds, a basketball court and a baseball field which we had not had in our school in Rome. This was mainly because of the lack of space living in central Rome. Of course, we had a football (soccer) field as that was Italy's national sport but we never had basketball or baseball facilities.

Back in Italy I loved all sports and I played football (soccer) as a "striker" and I was good at this. But here it was American football and baseball that were the kings of sports. I learned to play football and gave it everything I could in order to excel as I have always done in anything I ever undertook. We played street football in Italy which we didn't do here but that was fine by me as all else was very cool and I loved it!

I have to say that for the first four months, life at school, for me was mostly an existence in silence, as I couldn't speak or understand much of what was being said, which was very hard as I was a well-known talker (and I still am) but it was interesting, listening to the words my school friends used most frequently, words including, "like" and "cool" and other words they frequently added to a sentence. These and of course other words, of which there are many, but I can't repeat them here!

During those first months my sister and I went to language labs, elocution labs and other places to learn the language, sometimes three classes on the same day. We were both determined to learn the language as quickly as possible.

We were determined to do something to "make it here," whatever it took so we worked hard to make it happen. Seeing this as "hard" or "easy," was irrelevant, it was the end game that we were focused on and that was to speak and understand the language like a native.

This for me was everything as I was going to speak just like a local and I was going to make it no matter what! That was the determination I would need later on in my life I just didn't know it yet.

I never allowed the difficulty of doing something new to prevent me from succeeding.

Chapter 20

A Lesson Learned

Before my career was getting started, my father was having a hard time finding work in Hollywood. Here he was, even with his extensive film pedigree, and being nominated for a Golden Globe in Italy, now he was being treated like an unknown guy seemingly off the streets, because he was Italian!

He was now only able to get small parts as an Italian or in a Mexican movie but nothing even close to what he had done, as a movie star, in Italy. He couldn't play any lead roles because lead roles were white and English speaking, so every time he got a part it was as a chef, or as a bad guy or a hood, but nothing big at all and certainly nothing that would use his acting skills.

It was heartbreaking for me to see this and how he was being treated by the movie industry in Hollywood, when all he had done was good work and over such a long time, playing such a diverse range of parts. He found it hard to get cast as anything substantial, he was only getting small parts to play. I was so sad for him, but I couldn't let him know how I felt. It was incredibly depressing to see him calling people he had met before, people like Lee Majors, who I was a huge fan of, trying to find work for himself.

One day my father told me he had talked with Lee Majors and he had agreed to meet us. I loved him in *The Six Million Dollar Man,* which was my favorite Lee Majors work. My father and I went along to 20th Century Fox, where Lee had started filming *"The Fall Guy."*

We were waiting, as agreed, on the lot of *Star Wars* by a warehouse where he had agreed to come out and meet us. We were waiting for Lee to come out to meet us and waited for around four hours standing there hoping to see him, but he never came out!

I asked my father, "Where is he, he agreed to see us?" My father said, sadly, "He's not coming out son." Instead, Lee sent a PA, some four hours after we had arrived, to tell us he was too busy to see us. We had made the trip especially to see him, but the famous Lee Majors, my idol, up to that point, couldn't even be bothered to come out walking just a few steps, for a short time to meet us and it was a very short walk for him from the studio to where we were waiting, not even just to say hello. I knew my dad was deeply embarrassed and we walked away in silence with both of us feeling very disappointed.

I learned a lesson from that, a valuable lesson, that I would never ever behave like Lee Majors had to us and would always meet my fans, (if I ever had any) and I would never treat anyone, especially my fans, like this. I have never forgotten that lesson and I make sure I never treat anyone like Lee Majors treated us that day.

It's hard to forget the disappointment I saw in my father's face when he was simply trying to make me happy, by fixing it for me to meet my idol. Maybe Lee Majors was too busy that one afternoon to meet us, but whatever. We decided to give him the benefit of doubt.

I learned a valuable lesson from this, that I would always care about my fans!

Chapter 21

Working Hard

I was almost Sixteen now and we were living at Marina del Ray. I wanted to earn my own money and to be independent. I certainly didn't want my mom or dad to have to pay for me now, especially as I had left school. They had done more than enough to set Simonne and I on the right path to succeed.

I did many jobs to earn money and I wanted very much to stand on my own two feet and be independent. Back then, I did so many different things, I loved the challenge and the independence it brought me. I worked in warehouses, moving stock, I worked helping people to move their things and I was paid for my help. I was strong and liked doing manual work like this and I would do any odd job that people asked me to do.

I also worked as an usher at the local cinema the United Artists Theatre, as a ticket manager, then moved on as an assistant manager earning $3.75 an hour. I worked at Haagen-Dazs also, scooping out ice cream and I really didn't mind that at all. In fact, I often did several jobs simultaneously, but I loved it as I was earning money!

I got a job as a messenger driving around Beverly Hills in my first car, a white Honda Civic complete with sheepskin seat covers. I loved my first set of wheels, the car was all mine, I had bought it on my own.

It was reliable and got me to where I needed to get to, and I was always in a hurry.

My messenger job was mainly delivering film scripts to the offices of film executives and to agents, producers and directors and to many other individuals at all levels in the movie business. Some were famous at that time and some were names I didn't recognize or people who were not yet famous. I had a radio on my belt to get instant dispatches often while already on a delivery. I needed to work to pay for the insurance and gas to keep my little Honda going.

I would arrive at one address, running up the stairs, or in the elevator, grab the documents and leave as fast as possible to get my "package" to its destination in the fastest possible time, I was good at that. I knew Hollywood like the back of my hand and this was a busy time for me. I think if I wanted to, I could have been an excellent cab driver with all I knew about how to get to the many places I picked up or delivered to. I dreamed that one day I would have an agent represent me and maybe someone else would deliver scripts, contracts and storylines to me, one day.

If a package wasn't ready yet, or if the person I was delivering to, wasn't ready for me, I always had a newspaper with me to read the ads to see if there was the possibility for a new job. I didn't care how many jobs I had or how hard the work was. I was always on the lookout for my next opportunity to earn some cash. I was so busy with my day job as a messenger and my other jobs, that I really had no time for myself, despite this I knew I would be able to eventually get into the movie business one way or another. That was going to be my goal. I was determined to be that well-known actor to be just the same as all those I was delivering scripts on behalf of.

When we can see where our destiny leads, we do everything necessary to get there.

Chapter

My Family and My Racing Photos

This is a photo of my great grandparents kept in my family for over 100 years. It is a wedding group circa 1902, the couple 2nd right at the back, are my great grandparents.

The Sabato family. Four brothers and four sisters,
Antonio Sabato, Sr. 3rd from the right.

My grandfather, Nonno Giuseppe Sabato (in the white hat) with his friends. My middle name is also Giuseppe.

My grandfather Nonno Giuseppe on the beach.

My grandfather (my mother's father) forced into becoming a
circus act performing on a unicycle with my mother Yvonne, at
3 years old, doing acrobatics on his shoulders.

My mother's parents William and Magda Saghy, the
photo was taken in Prague.

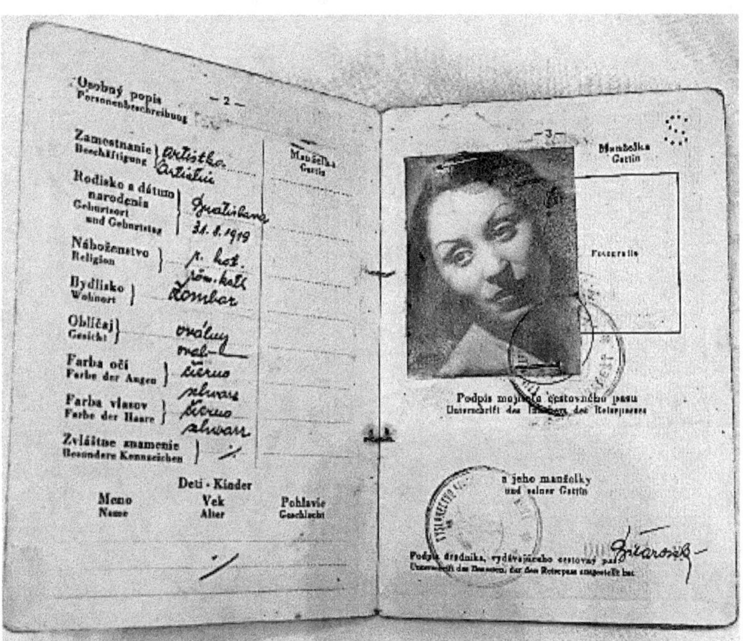

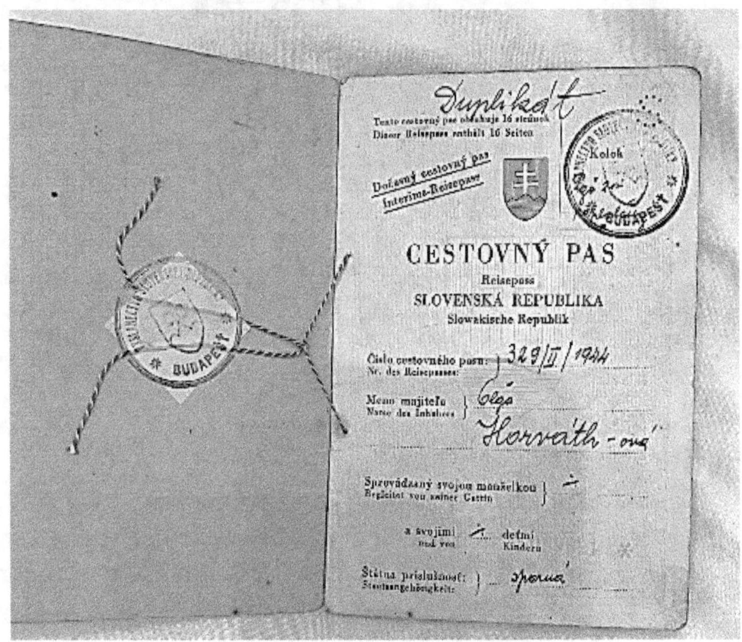

My grandmother's forged passport, in 1944, that she used to escape the Nazis, in Czechoslovakia.

My mother's father, William Saghy our grandfather, with my sister, Simonne (right) with me at Theresienstadt Concentration Camp in Czechoslovakia. This visit meant a lot to us both having lost our great grandparents to the death camp at Auschwitz.

These documents from the Red Cross show the train number, the carriage, the date and travel information that took my mother's grandparents on, what they did not know was to be, their last journey to Auschwitz.

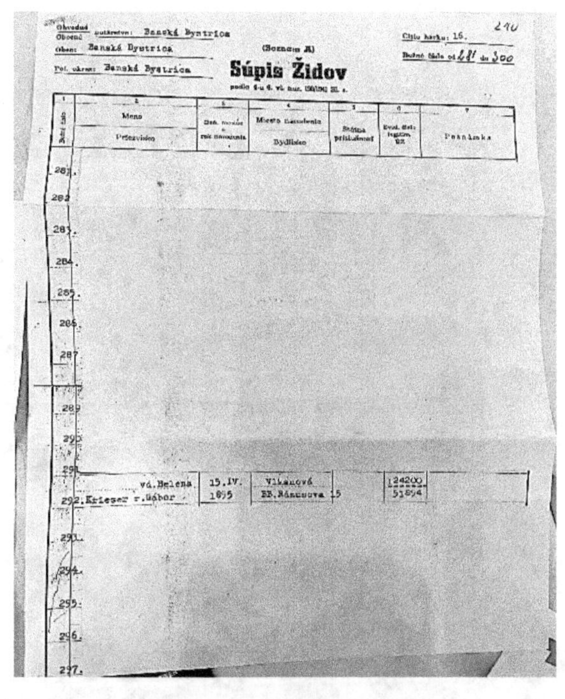

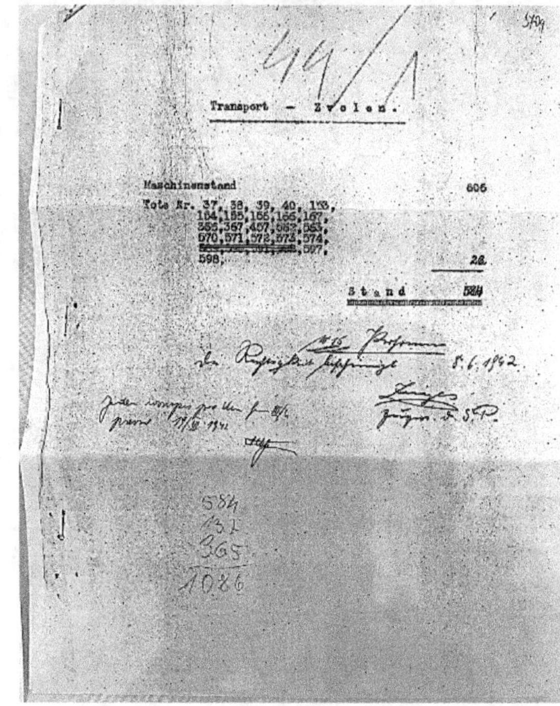

My mother, in front, with her parents Magda and William Saghy. The blonde woman was a friend at the time.

Me at 8 years old with my sister Simonne,
on our family's boat.

Me and my sister Simonne with
our father Antonio Sabato, Sr.

My father Antonio Sabato, Sr. on
an early modeling shoot. We looked
so much alike.

A PR photo shoot of me, trackside at Willow
Springs Racetrack.

The cover of my first book,

No Excuses.

From my racing days, I'm trackside at Willow Springs, CA.

With Formula 1 racing legend Michael Schumacher.

With racing car driver and founder of
the Williams Formula 1 team, Sir Frank
Williams.

This was the last day of filming *Grace by Night*. We went through a lot during the filming, but it was an amazing spiritual and physical journey.

With Katia, one of my favorite photos.

My father, Antonio Sabato, Sr.

With my racing Porsche at Indianapolis Motor Speedway in 2002.

Me with legendary Formula 1 racing
driver the late Niki Lauda.

I'm in a go kart at Willow Springs racetrack. My father was with me at this race.

On the movie set, *Five del Condor*, with my father.

My father in the movie *Grand Prix*.

With Mom, my sister Simonne and my daughter Mina. My son Jack is hiding in the bushes.

With my daughter Mina.

With my son Antonio Sabato III. His real name is
Antonio Kamakanalohamaikalani (Hawaiian).

Chapter 22

My First Movie Role

My very first role in the movie industry was working on a CBS "*School Break*" series, in 1990, directed by Mario Van Peebles. I was in an episode called "*Malcolm Takes a Shot.*" I was a "stand in" for John Clair who was playing Malcolm Jones at that time in one of these "after school specials" for kids to watch when they got home from school. These movies were based on education and contained real educational subjects. They had good vibes and were great to watch for school children.

Tony Lo Bianco played the coach and he and I have remained friends ever since then but not because of movies. He and I do a lot of work with the National American Italian Foundation, (NAIF) where we meet every year to help Italians in, or wanting to get into, the entertainment business in any capacity. I loved helping out with this organization because I remember how hard it was for me to break into movies.

I was getting paid three hundred bucks a week, which for me back then was a very good wage. I drove to the set and spent time with the crew, getting to know as much as I could about the technical side of the movie industry and I loved it. I was gradually getting into the movie business and I felt I was slowly getting to where I had planned to be as a schoolboy.

Early Days with My Father

My movie career was just taking off I landed roles in three Italian movies, only a few years after arriving in California, this was 1988 to 1991 and started when I was 17 years old.

I made three Italian films. One of these films was very important in Italy. It was *"Si non avessi L'amore" made* in 1991 the film followed the last year of Pier Giorgio Frassati, a wealthy Italian, who led such a unique life. He was the son of the wealthy owners of the Italian newspaper *La Stampa* who lived between 1901 and 1925. Pier Giorgio, although very wealthy, spent his life helping the poor and the film was shown in a special viewing to Pope John Paul II on Christmas Eve 2991, which is a very special day in the Papal calendar. Was offered the role and I played the lead role of Pier Giorgia. The reason it was in a special showing to the Pope was because the Holy See was considering canonizing Pier Giorgio for his lifetime of helping the poor. The film was also shown on the Italian national TV channel Rai1.

I went back to Italy to finish the movie I was in, "Arizona Road" which was now moving production from the US. to Italy and it was exciting for me. I was heading back to my home country but this time as a professional actor at nineteen years old. It wasn't my agent who did the work for me but my father! He was still very well-known and had so many connections in the movie business there and he always had my back.

I traveled back to Italy with my father, who was helping me with my lines and we were working on the script together. It was a great time for me, to be working with him on something that, with his sixty -five movies, he was an expert at. He taught me well and I remember all his lessons even now.

Papa was showing me how to do the part, things I should be aware of, lighting, stagecraft, how to say my lines which way to face and everything he had learned from his years in the movie business. He knew so much about acting and the industry. Me? I was lucky I could act in Italian and English. I could speak both very well and not many in the industry can do this. However, while I was filming there, I was treated very badly by the director of that film. After seeing what was happening, my father told the director, "Hey if you don't look after my son, we're going to walk."

What a dad I had, always looking after my interests! In Italy, they don't do things like they do in Hollywood. They can keep you for exceptionally long hours, no overtime, no extra pay, nothing. It was very long, hard hours of work in the Italian film industry. I didn't mind the hard work, but the long hours doing nothing were a problem. However, these were very precious moments for me working with my father, my very own personal and expert coach, one-on-one showing me and helping me with all I needed to know to do the best performance I could.

I will never forget all the help and guidance Papa gave me when I was just starting out as an actor and, if not for his help, I may never have got the start I needed in those early days of my career. Being an actor in Hollywood is a highly competitive business and all the help I had helped me to at least get my foot in the door to land some of those early roles. Thanks Papa, I loved those precious times we had together just you and me and I remember everything you taught me and the fun we had while you were my teacher.

I treasure the many lessons my Papa gave me, as I believe without his wisdom and time, I could never have succeeded.

Chapter 23

Janet Jackson

It was 1990, when I was scouring the ads as I always did, looking for auditions, to see what was around when I came across an ad looking for bikers needed for a music video. I knew I had no leathers and certainly wasn't a biker, but I decided to do the audition anyway. I went to the location and when I got there, there were hundreds of "Biker Dudes" and I was the only person there who wasn't. We had to do a dance routine to a piece of music Janet Jackson had just recorded, so I did just that, I danced. Then I was asked to say a few words to Janet, as if I was standing next to her for the first time for the video.

I looked directly at the camera and told her I loved her music and I liked her too and couldn't wait to meet her. I went away after that audition and thought nothing more about it.

A few days later I got a call from the agency saying I had the part. It paid three hundred dollars and I was to go to a Dry Lakebed, just outside Lancaster in California, a spot I knew well as I had been there many times before.

I drove there in my little white Honda and at first, I couldn't see anything like a film crew, so I started to drive around. I eventually found the trucks and film crew way over the other side of Dry Lakebed. While I was waiting around, getting to know the crew and asking if I could help move stuff around, the photographer who was shooting the scene, Herb Ritts, came over and took me to one side and said, "I have someone for you to meet."

As instructed by Herb, I waited by the corner of some trucks, to see who it was that I was supposed to meet. After a few minutes, Janet Jackson came around the corner. I was stunned to see her face to face and I didn't know what to say. She came right up to me and gave me a big hug; I hugged her back and, just like that, we began working together.

Janet was tiny in stature but huge in reputation and she was to me a really great person to talk to. We got along very well as we started to do the filming. The video, was for her single *"Love Will Never Do (without you)."*

The music video was directed by photographer, Herb Ritts and choreographed by Ritts, with Janet Jackson and Tina Landon. I was featured along with actor Djimon Hounsou and got a close-up dancing and moving with Janet Jackson. The video was filmed on the Dry Lakebed, in beautiful hot sunny weather with not a cloud in the sky.

Djimon was a former Calvin Klein underwear model and was represented by Albertto's Models." I remember Djimon's deep voice and he and I were filmed in the video for her production. Djimon went on into acting and was nominated for an Oscar in *"Blood Diamond,"* I saw that movie and Djimon was superb! I loved the end of that movie when he arrives to do a speech at a huge convention to outlaw "Blood Diamonds." That film really moved me.

I had never made a music video before and working with Janet Jackson, was a very cool experience for me. She was the consummate professional performer, she made it easy for me to work with her, helping me with each scene. The legendary Herb Albert played trumpet in the backing track.

We got along very well so after the album was released, while she was performing it live on stage, in LA and again in Las Vegas, she called me to ask me to appear on stage with her to perform that song, as we had done in her music video.

So, I went on-stage to meet her and we would hug on stage in front of some thirty thousand of her fans. I was just eighteen then and all the attention was exhilarating and overwhelming, but Janet made me feel comfortable being with her with her cool professionalism in front of the largest audience I had ever been in front of.

I saw her again later at the World Music Awards when I was presenting an award in Monaco, we hung out together and we were friends. We reminisced about making that video which was for me the high point in my career. Her video, filmed by Herb Ritts, won so many awards and it was one of the best music videos in the world at that time. It was really beautifully filmed and was nominated for Best Choreography and Best Art Direction at the 1991 MTV Video Music Awards.

It ranked 13 on *Rolling Stone's 100 Top Music Videos*, it made number 72 on VH1's 100 Greatest Videos and 88 on MTV's 100 Greatest Videos Ever Made, thanks to the skill of our late friend Herb Ritts together with Janet Jackson.

I loved doing it and after Janet's song was released, we kept in contact. In her stage routine we aligned her performance closely to what we had done in the video promoting it. I performed with Janet live on stage and people saw that we had a connection. She was a true professional.

Janet and I got on very well as friends and it was thanks to me being seen in that Janet Jackson video that I became well-known all over the world if only for how I looked, as videoed by Herb Ritts, as no one then knew my name, only my part in her video. But what a start to a career, being filmed by the world's best and dancing with one of the most famous singers, Janet Jackson.

Herb Ritts and Janet Jackson were true professionals who I was privileged to work with and learn from and we had fun working together.

Chapter 24

Modeling

When I was living in New York and scouring the Ads pages in the newspapers, as I always did whenever I had the chance, I found an ad in the *"Venice Magazine,"* from a photographer looking for male models. The job paid ten bucks an hour, so I called the studio and went along to meet the photographer to see if this was a real opportunity and I saw that he was legit.

I got the job and what helped me was all the teaching my parents had given me about hard work and having a good work ethic. I knew what was required of me and I made sure I did what I was supposed to do. They took loads of photographs of me and one day after looking at all my photos they said, "maybe you can model!" This was something I hadn't thought about, as at that time ten bucks an hour was what I worked for, but what the heck, why not? I started doing various layouts for them and best of all I was getting paid for doing them.

After seeing how I looked in their many photos, they said, "Tell you what, were going to send these photos to a modeling agency." The agency was called, "Omar's Men," with offices in LA and New York. They were a big agency and, as I was to find out, they were highly respected in the world of modeling.

They were always looking for potential models and the agency was owned by Omar **Albertto**. Anyway, I called them and went along for an interview. After my portfolio shots were completed, they called me to let me know they thought I had the "look" and they told me they wanted to represent me, which was fine by me.

When I went to their LA offices I saw the walls there were filled with photos of models many of whom I had seen in magazines and some I had seen on TV and as I was to find out "Albertto's" had been used in advertising and PR in campaigns for Gucci, **Versace, Armani, Ralph Lauren, Dolce & Gabbana and many others. They were the real thing!**

We then did a test photo shoot with me in different poses, for lighting and clothing. Their work was exceptional, they made me look great (far better than I thought I looked). The shots came out well and I did several layouts for them which they sent out to advertising, PR and other modeling agencies.

They gave me work earning fifty bucks here, sixty bucks there and it was interesting, getting paid for basically standing and sitting round. I was finally making it on my own, earning my own money and I was having fun doing the work. They told me they had an office in New York and said I should go there if I wanted more work.

They said they could hook me up with better work in New York and maybe I could get into some magazines. They said I might even be able to make as much as three hundred bucks a week! Well at that time and compared to my, one sandwich each day cut in four, making four almost square meals (which was all I could afford) this was more than I could imagine earning.

They found me a job for *The New York Times,* who were looking for people to model for *Macy's* and *J C Penny.* They paid me three hundred dollars up front. I packed my bags to leave for New York. I even had an agent there who could find me work so off I went.

When I arrived, I went to the agency and they put me up in an apartment they used for their models. The apartment was on the west side of Manhattan in New York. The apartment had no hot water and no cooling, it was summer, but it was perfect for me at that time and living there allowed me to save my money.

I managed to live on just twenty bucks a week. With my twenty bucks I was able to go to the deli and buy their big sandwiches, cut them into four pieces making each one last a whole day as I had done before, but now it was because I wanted to save my money not because I couldn't afford much.

I remember at that time I was always hungry, but I was making it on the money I was being paid. My mom often told me I ate like a vacuum cleaner! The modeling work at that time, as I saw it, was really a woman's world, but I thought maybe I can do this for a while until something better comes along. Little did I know that modeling would become part of my career later in my life.

I followed in my parents' footsteps and did whatever it took earning my own money to become independent.

Chapter 25

Tully Jensen

I was still on the books with Omar's Models when I saw, in their offices, many photos on the walls of other models they were working with. One model I liked in particular that caught my eye was Tully Jensen and I wanted to meet her. In 1991 we did finally meet and when I moved to New York Tully let me stay at her apartment for three months, which helped me to get started there.

That time in my life was fantastic, there weren't enough hours in the day for me to do all I wanted to get done.

Tully and I married the following year in 1992 I was 20 years old, but soon afterwards we both came to the realization that our marriage was not going to work out and I really wasn't ready to make a commitment like this, nor was I suited to marriage to anyone for that matter, at that time.

Tully and I didn't get along after we were married and it only got worse for both of us as time went on. Sometimes the chemistry is wrong and there is nothing we can do about it and when that became apparent as it did with Tully and me, it was time for us both to move on. It doesn't make either of us bad people, but it simply meant we were not destined to spend our lives together.

After only five months we divorced so we could both move on with our lives. My acting career was just beginning and I wanted to focus on that and nothing else. I was sad that divorce was the outcome for Tully and me, but we could do nothing else and we both moved on with our lives.

Recognizing incompatibility means making changes sooner than later.

Chapter 26

Winning Auditions

I needed to learn more about my craft, so I started acting classes with Nina Foch. Nina Foch played the wealthy lady in *"An American in Paris"* with Gene Kelly. She has sadly now passed away but back then, she taught me the "acting technique," which I really needed to learn and Nina was an exceptional teacher.

I knew I had to learn more if I was going to win auditions for better movies and TV shows. My dad was my manager and helped me a lot, teaching me how to watch my back and the pitfalls of bad contracts.

Nina had the ability to steal scenes that she was in even if those scenes were with the absolute best actors and actresses she worked with. She had such a strong character and was also known for her great with. She told me, "If you want to make it in acting and win auditions, you need to be in one of my Master Acting classes." So, I did just that and I was surrounded by people who were a lot older than me, but I didn't care as long as she was willing to teach me what I needed to know I was more than willing and driven to learn.

Anyway, in the meantime, my father who was in LA, looking for work, called me to tell me he had been in touch with one of his friends who was about to make a movie in Savanna Georgia. It was a low budget Italian film to be shot in English. They wanted me to make a promo trailer, so together my dad and I put one together and sent it to them. They liked it and I landed a role in the movie. I was still living in New York and flew down to Savanna to start work on the movie for which they paid me five thousand bucks wow! The movie was called *"Karate Rock,"*

I had my own hotel room and I was acting in a real movie! I had more money than I had ever earned before and I was having the time of my life! I worked extremely hard and was learning more about acting in a real movie with other actors, doing my own stunts and doing my very best.

The movie was not to be a huge box office success, probably because all the actors, like me, were all new to acting. The crew was only three people, the director, the producer, who was also the cameraman and one more, who was the assistant. But despite this and despite the fact that it was not such a good film, it got me into the movie business, which was ultimately my goal.

The producer told me that if I worked hard in this movie maybe they would put me in a second movie that was to follow. The second movie was to be shot in Arizona and would be mine to do, but only if I did well with this first one.

They liked my part in that first film, *"Karate Rock"* and I landed the second acting role also. The film was called *"Arizona Road, escape from Kayenta"* (my father came up with that name). All the hard work I had done for their first movie led to me landing the role, as they had promised, for their second film. At this point so early in my career I had no idea what was to be a good movie or a bad movie but then, my career was just getting started.

Enter Jagger Cates

After that first movie, I flew back to Los Angeles and because I had my first movie part, I was able to make a short sample clip from the film, which we sent to an agent my father knew. When learning our craft, we have to take the rough with the smooth it is part of the process and for me it was exciting to be part of making movies even if that movie wasn't what I hoped it would be.

With the short clip from my movie "Karate Rock" we were able to send it out to agencies around Hollywood. I now had an agent who had managed to set up a meeting for me with the casting director of "*General Hospital*" and I went to meet him, for an audition at the ABC studios on Prospect. My meeting was for a role in a TV series and I was to go to the set where they were filming. I will talk later about this TV series and the role I auditioned for.

I auditioned many times for a role in the series and the part I was auditioning for was initially for a character called "Ricky," In the series *General Hospital*. What I did know was that I wanted it so badly, but after several auditions I didn't land that part. I was heartbroken but, as my father told me many times, "that's the movie business son, you'll have many more misses than hits." One thing I had to get used to was not landing roles that I auditioned for and being rejected was part of the process. Actors must have a thick skin to deal with the many rejections they will have along the way.

But later, while I was learning my craft (we never stop learning), I was invited to another screen test for *General Hospital* for the part of "*John Jagger Cates*." For this role I had determined that no one was going to take this away from me. I worked so hard on it and auditioned at least ten times for the part. Each audition was different from the last.

The Friday following the last audition, I was waiting all day for a call and I knew having done so many auditions I must be in with a chance.

They told me I wouldn't know until the following Monday. As you can imagine, I was a bundle of nerves all that weekend.

It was now 1992, I was 20 years old and it was on the following Monday when I got the call at 10am while I was staying at my parents' town house and my sister was in the room next door. When I heard the news that I had at last, landed the role, I was jumping up and down on the bed and screaming, "I did it I did it." I broke the bed, but it didn't matter I now had a real part in a well-known and popular TV drama.

But now, I also had no bed to sleep in (I had broken it jumping up and down). It didn't matter to me, all I cared about was that I had done it! My acting classes had helped me and if it wasn't for all that hard work, the help and the training I received, from Jay, Nina, Howard, the Executive Producer and especially the help I received from my father, I would maybe still be a messenger boy! I had no idea how this role would change my life.

I went to work immediately to perform the role as *Jagger Cates* and it was to last for three years. I worked each day with the Executive Producer, who was my boss and we worked very well together along with the other members of the cast. Her direction for me in the series as *John Jagger Cates* led my part to become one of the biggest and most recognizable character names of all time in soaps. That was me!

Things were looking up and around this time, after my role in *General Hospital* my mother now owned a successful restaurant in Beverley Hills called "Triloussa" after she sold it, she opened another restaurant called "Sabato Cucina" (Sabato's Kitchen) South of Wilshire on Beverley Drive. Big agents came on Monday nights which was party night with DJ's and dozens of Harley Davidson's parked along the road. We were doing fine now financially, mainly because of my mom's restaurant business. Mom is a genius at business.

My part in *General Hospital* meant we trained for each and every scene, before it was filmed, to make it perfect and to make sure when we were on camera we utilized the time effectively. It was hard and often repetitive work, but that was what was required and was the reason the series became so popular. In fact, while I was on the show it jumped from seventh to second most popular TV Soap. I was getting up at 4am doing my workouts before my "day job" going onto the set to be *Jagger Cates* once again.

We were developing the role of *Jagger Cates* into a huge success and I was under the coaching of Jay Goldenberg, during my role in *General Hospital*. Jay introduced me to Howard Fine, who had a well-known acting and speech school in Los Angeles. I joined his class and now I was learning my art and taking lessons from the best in the business and I loved it.

It wasn't cheap and my mom and dad had to save up to pay for my acting lessons. My mom took on three jobs for me to attend acting classes. I also went to classes at The Stella Adler Studio where there were several people there who helped me by showing me what I needed to know to become a good actor. I had been told by other actors that if I did soaps, I would never get major film roles and vice versa. But for me acting was working and I wanted to work as much as I could.

Enter Steven Spielberg

I was auditioning for other roles while I was playing Jagger Cates as I wanted to become an actor in movies as well as being in TV shows. There was an upcoming TV show called "*Earth 2*" a new Steven Spielberg project. It was the biggest TV show at the time. I was offered a role in this new project along with a guarantee of being in the entire season. As a result, I had to think now, do I stay or do I go, to begin a new project and leave this most successful show *General*

Hospital. I made the difficult decision to move on from *General Hospital* after 2 years, because I didn't want to become typecast as a soap star. The new show was to be a pilot and I had the opportunity to work on Spielberg's new TV series. I had always wanted to work with Steven Spielberg and now I had the opportunity.

On my final day of filming for *General Hospital* I rode my Harley Davidson on to the set and my very last scene was me riding my Harley off into the sunset with my co-star, Karen played by Cari Shayne. Together we rode off the set just as it was now in real life. I said my goodbyes and I headed straight over to New Mexico to begin filming on *Earth 2.*

We can never guess what else might have been, had I made a different choice, but this was my decision and mine alone and I left *General Hospital* for my new role in *Earth 2* in 1994 with some regrets.

However, twenty-five years later I am constantly asked," when will I be returning as *to "General Hospital"* In the series. *Jagger Cates* was never killed off, so I hoped maybe one day he will return. If he does, he would probably be a little older and a lot wiser than he was back then.

In part, my book is a message about moving on past all that lie throes at us. My family had to do this, many times, from Hungary, from Czechoslovakia and from Italy in our past.

I moved on from *General Hospital* for a part in what was supposed to be a blockbuster series, called *"Earth 2,"* produced by Steven Spielberg, but none of us can foresee what the public choose as something they want to watch.

As it turned out the movie did not do well in the ratings she and the box office. Who knows if I would make the same choice if offered a similar role again, but as they say, "Hindsight is twenty-twenty!"

Personal success is when we can look back at what we have done and know we did something right. For me Jagger Cates was something right!

Chapter 27

Calvin Klein

I was in a movie called *"If Looks Could Kill"* a 1996 made for TV movie about a criminal called John Hawkins, who I played as the lead role of John Hawkins. The film was based on his life as a notoriously elusive criminal who was profiled on the TV series "America's Most Wanted." I had played the lead and it was, for me, an intriguing role to play. To learn about someone like him who, thankfully, I would never ever meet in my life and now to be playing him in a movie was interesting and a little scary.

Little did I know, at the time, that this movie, was to change my life. It was the movie that the fashion icon Calvin Klein saw me in and wanted to meet me. A meeting was arranged and I went to meet him in New York. We talked and he told me he was interested to see how I would look as his model and as a representative for his men's underwear line.

He went to great lengths to explain that this was to be a lifestyle change for me and would involve many photo shoots in studios and in locations, perhaps all over the world. He went on to tell me about the kind of work I would be doing for him to make sure I was OK with this as it would be a change of direction for me and I have to say, I was excited at this incredible opportunity. I could hardly believe that he saw me in that dark horror movie and had wanted to meet me.

As we talked about what he wanted we got on very well and I knew we could work well together. He then asked me if I minded wearing his line of men's underwear, of course I said yes I wouldn't mind at all though I had little idea what it would entail for me.

I did my first photo shoot for Calvin Klein with the famous photographer Wayne Maser and I have to say his photographs of me were spectacular. He had created ad campaigns for Calvin Klein and DKNY among others and photographed cover pages for such well-known magazines as Harper's Bazaar, Marie Claire, Vanity Fair, GQ, and Esquire. He was very much in demand for his portraits of many present-day legends. These included Johnny Depp, Rob Lowe, Madonna, Mariah Carey, Clint Eastwood, Brigitte Nielsen, Whitney Houston, Angelina Jolie and Elizabeth Taylor. The campaign he shot with me went global and Calvin was very happy with me and how I looked representing his world-famous fashion line.

The second campaign I did was shot by Herb Ritts in Malibu and it was now the second time I had the opportunity to work with Herb. He was known for his photographs of Ronald Reagan, Madonna, Richard Gere, David Bowie, Michael Jackson and many more well-known figures. In fact, Herb's work was a who's who of pop culture and the list goes on and on. His specialty like Wayne's, was shooting in high contrast black and white.

Our third campaign was shot in New York by Kelly Klein who was married to Calvin Klein, at that time. Kelly's photos were creative as well and I saw that each of these incredible photographers had a different style.

I did more campaigns for Calvin Klein than anyone else had ever done and I was having the time of my life working with Calvin! I can't say it was hard work though, but I had to look perfect for every shot, my hair, my body, my face, all had to be precisely as the photographer wanted it for this high-definition photographic work, with me as his "perfect image."

On The Catwalk

Working with Calvin meant that I had to do several fashion shows and this meant I would be on the catwalk. I never felt comfortable when I was on the Catwalk because I didn't feel that I belonged there with these, most beautiful people in the world, who all looked so perfect. Despite all I was doing with Calvin Klein, I was and still am quite shy. I was never too happy with the way I looked when I was with all these professional and perfectly built beautiful models.

Privately, I felt I didn't belong there on the Catwalk, but my job was my job and I did what I was required to do, after all, I was now a professional model. Many people feel the same about themselves, I felt like an ordinary person who was just lucky to be there. It was this feeling that would later drive me to write my book, *"No Excuses"* so others, I hoped, would do as I had done to look after themselves as I had learned to do.

As I saw it, modeling was similar to acting, but without any words and instead of moving around saying my lines my, "acting" was in stills, and in my expression as I moved from one pose to another and leaving it to the photographer's vision. In some ways the photographer was the same as a movie director.

A photograph is a split-second moment in our lives and is a moment captured in a single frame that can never be repeated.

Chapter 28

Truth or Dare

It was through my friendship with Herb Ritts and the incredible photos he took of me for Calvin Klein that I met Madonna. She had seen the video Herb filmed for Janet Jackson's hit, *"Love Will Never Do (Without You)*. Madonna had seen it, back in 1991 and wanted to meet me.

Although millions of people had seen me, all over the world in her video, no one knew my name at that time, there was little social media either so finding out who's who, back then, meant calling around to friends and contacts.

I was spending a lot of time with Herb Ritts at that time and Madonna was at the top of her game, as she still is. She was doing so much on TV, in movies and her music career with hit after hit, it seemed everything she did turned to gold! At the same time her documentary "Truth or Dare" had recently been released and of course that was a huge hit as well.

Immediately after making Janet's video, I had gone to Italy to make two films, so I had little idea what was going on back in the U.S. It was sometime later when people found out who I was, from my Janet Jackson video, that I started to get a lot more work.

Anyway, Madonna obtained my number from Peter Savic, my hairdresser, who did my hair for the video shoot and he was friends with Madonna as well as with Herb. He gave her my number and told me she had been wanting to contact me. I told him where I usually hung out and a short time after my conversation with Peter, she called me, out of the blue! When I answered the phone, she simply said, "Hi It's me Madonna, I would love to meet you. Would you like to come to New York so we can meet up?" I was surprised to get that call and said, "Sure I can come to New York." Like I was going to say no to Madonna, at that time when I was still relatively unknown!

Partying with Madonna

She invited me to a party, in New York, and she was there with some of her friends, including Rupert Everett. As the party was in full swing, she decided we should play the game, "Truth or Dare" which was very appropriate at that time because her movie of the same name had just been released.

We all agreed, to play the game and the first "dare" was from Madonna who said, "I dare Antonio to kiss Rupert!" Now I am not gay, ok, but a dare is a dare and I certainly was not going to ruin the game just as it had begun, so I kissed Rupert Everett! I had never ever kissed a man before and I can tell you I have no intention of ever doing it again, but for that game, it was ok and it was after all a dare.

I thought Madonna was testing me to see if I was someone she wanted to have around. Game on and when it was my turn, to come up with a truth or dare. I thought OK, you want to play that game and so I dared Madonna to "get it on" with me right then and there despite never having met her before that night! I then I stood up and went over and sat down on the couch right next to her and we started kissing and I mean really kissing.

Everything went quiet for a moment with everyone waiting to see if there would be any reaction. But Madonna kissed me right back, then everyone was now whistling and cheering, while I was still kissing

Madonna! I looked at her, raising one eyebrow as if to say, "did I pass your test?" After that Madonna and I hung out during that entire summer of 1991.

While we were hanging out together that summer, in New York where she was living at the time, the Paparazzi were there too every single day outside her apartment. I don't know to this day how she copes with their intrusive behavior every single day, but she did and she managed it well, certainly better than I could have. To avoid them seeing me I used the side entrance and it worked, they never saw me enter or leave and we were never an item together to reach the news, which was how we wanted it.

No one ever took any photos of me going in and out of Madonna's apartment block and there were no photographs or articles about the two of us, in any of the press, so our secret was safe. Our relationship, as friends, was very private and nothing was ever in the press or out in public, until now. Madonna and I hung out that summer, it was not a long relationship but it was fun while it lasted.

Madonna is very petite, very polite and I liked her immediately. She was very straight forward and very confident and why not? She was the biggest female star in the world and she still is!

Sometime later, I took my family skiing to Big Bear Mountain and I told my mom I had met Madonna, she was surprised as nothing had been mentioned at all and I was happy we had beaten the press. I knew I could trust that my mom would never tell a soul and she never did. Madonna was a kind person and we had a great time together doing very ordinary things. I can honestly say I learned a lot about women from being with Madonna and I still think back to that "one hot" summer with "Hot" Madonna, in 1991.

We kept our relationship secret, very successfully. The first time I ever mentioned our relationship was not long ago, but nevertheless it was a long time after we dated.

Underneath the fame and glitz Madonna is a very real person, as I found out then, no bells and whistles just a normal truly kind (and beautiful) person.

Chapter 29

Times Square

I had been working for Calvin Klein for around 3 years, I was fit and had a good physique, but Calvin did not want a "body builder" type of physique like Arnold Schwarzenegger, he wanted a completely natural trim, sculptured body with a look that people seeing me could identify with. Whereas a body builder type of body-shape was not something that would sell fashionable clothing.

One thing though, I had tattoos and back at that time there were no Calvin Klein models who had tattoos. Even Mark Wahlberg, modeling with Kate Moss, at that time, had to have his tattoos covered for the photo shoot. Then there was me, about to be in the big game representing Calvin Klein, with Asian signs and all sorts of art on my body, but they decided to let this go.

In 1996 while modeling for Calvin Klein, he placed my photo on a ninety-foot billboard overlooking Times Square in New York! That photograph was taken by Herb Ritts. A photo of that event is here in my book taken by my mom Yvonne.

I went to New York to unveil the billboard amid all the paparazzi and news media and I took my mother with me. She was so proud of all I had accomplished and loved that I was working with the famous Calvin Klein. It was an exciting time for us both. The billboard showed me in Underwear and it was hard to imagine how many millions of people would see me in my undies, even if they were white Calvin Klein brand!

My mother was so happy standing next to me as I unveiled the billboard amidst the cheer of a huge crowd of thousands who had all come to see me unveil that famous image of me. I was also delighted because I had done something to make my mom proud of me. In a New York Times article, I was referred to as a "Michael Angelo statue," well, I don't know about that, but it was Herb's skill with the camera lens and his perfection with lighting that make me look very good!

I was very close to my mother and always have been, so her telling me that she was proud of what I had accomplished made me very happy and was the "icing on the cake" for me.

Working with Calvin Klein was a real honor and we got on very well, we had become friends. He had me in shows as a "catwalk" model and in PR activities all over the world and my career really took off under his guidance.

I had never seen myself as a model and I wasn't sure at first that I could be because, believe it or not I, as I said before I was a very shy person. It eventually became three years of fast-moving action with interviews, PR work, travel, and celebrity appearances all over the world. Herb Ritts' photos of me caused a sensation and many of his photos appeared in almost every magazine along with hundreds of billboards throughout the world. I had reached the top as a model!

Working for and with the famous Calvin Klein was a very uplifting experience, what a true professional he really was. His vision, for all the work I was fortunate enough to do for him, was precise in explaining what he wanted and how he wanted each photo to look. I found Calvin to be straightforward, extremely hard working, graceful and a fun person to be with. I also knew that I had his trust and he had mine, which was important for a great working relationship.

Calvin Klein and I became friends and we still are, I value all he taught me in my career. Working with him and the valuable lessons I learned, about professionalism, I took with me, onwards, with my career and even now I recall all he taught me.

His insistence on professionalism, dedication and a strong professional work ethic, at all times, was a life lesson for me. His views on work were matched with my own, as my father and mother had always taught me. My father always said, "If they need you there at 6am, make sure you get there at 5am." I made sure that whenever I could, I did just that!

My work with Calvin Klein came to a natural close after three exciting years. Thank you, Calvin Klein, for the opportunity and all I learned from working with you.

I knew if I did nothing else, I did this with you, Calvin Klein and I had the time of my life!

Chapter 30

Versace and Ghosts

I **was in** a campaign with Gianni Versace, where they used two photos out of all the photos they took of me. Versace had many more famous and better-known models than me at that time. It was Herb Ritts who got me that job after working together on the Janet Jackson video. I was living in New York and they flew me to Hawaii for the shoot that summer to model their new line in swimsuits.

We were doing the photo shoot in Kona; the big island and I was sharing a large apartment with several other models. There were around six or seven of us at the time and I was sharing a room with one of the other models.

Sometime later, after I turned the lights off to go to sleep, when later that night my roommate switched the lights back on and started shouting, "I've just seen a ghost!" He was very animated and went on telling me he was seeing all these people, ghosts, singing and dancing in what appeared to be a renaissance period and not present day. He was telling me he saw people dancing on my bed!

I looked at him thinking, is this guy on something, is he high or what? I asked him, "what the hell are you talking about?" I had just been woken up in the middle of the night after a hard day's work modeling. He said, "No, no I'm not kidding I'm actually seeing these people right here, in this room and they are real, as real to me as you are right here."

I listened to him and told him he was imagining things and we had to get back to sleep. I looked around for any signs, movements or shadows, damn! He had me wondering as well! But I could tell from how he was behaving that he believed what he saw was real and was, in his mind, telling the truth, which disturbed me even more! We turned the lights off, but he saw the ghosts again and switched the lights back on again after a few minutes.

He quickly left the room saying," I'm not sleeping in there anymore!" and went to another room, where he started saying the same things, but this time the other model, who was now sharing the room with him, now saw them too!

I was wide awake now and was intrigued to find out more. So I went downstairs to the lobby, as I was now growing concerned about what the hell was going on in that hotel. I spoke to the concierge at the front desk and asked him if this had ever happened before. He told me yes, many times and as I was to find out, the hotel had been built on top of a burial ground! I never saw ghosts though, no matter how hard I tried to focus, thinking that was the way to see them. I had always wanted to see a ghost, but it was not going to happen for me that night.

By now I believed that what they had both seen, they maybe thought was real, so I went back to my room and focused on trying to see something, but I didn't see a thing. So, I went back to sleep and nothing further happened in my room.

There are many things all around us that we will never see, no matter how hard we look!

Chapter 31

Maximum Exposure

Around that time, I was on the cover of the TV Guide and I was the first soap actor to make it onto the *Arsenio Hall Show,* which was the biggest TV show at that time and was seen by millions. This was an exceptionally big deal for anyone at that time, as it was for me. He had the biggest stars on his show and now I was also appearing on his show as well. I have to admit that I didn't see myself as any kind of big star but who cares, I was happy to be invited onto Arsenio's show. It was, as I saw it, a rubber stamp of my success at the time.

I was in famous company then and before I was asked onto his show people I knew said to me "You'll never get on Arsenio Hall, but I did and the more people tried to play down all I was doing the harder I worked to prove them wrong. I learned that from my father. If I was to be a success, I had to do it myself, so I met with PR agencies and photographers to do shoots with other agents and did all I could to promote myself after all it was up to me to make sure I did all I could to continue working.

I had a vision of where I wanted to be and I understood all the things I needed to do to get there. I didn't want to be in soap operas all my life but of course I was very lucky to have had the exposure and to have learned so much from the cast, writers and direction I worked with. It was that experience that taught me so much but I wanted to be in mainstream movies and TV shows as well.

For the three years, from 1992 to 1995 I worked as hard as I could and I was nominated for the "Soap Opera Awards" as a result. I was invited to attend the Emmy's and many other events making personal celebrity appearances. I was on the cover of many magazines and my appearance drew hundreds of fans everywhere I went.

In fact, I sold millions of dollars' worth of news media, magazines, show ratings and many things I never knew about, with everything I was asked to do. But that, as they say that is show biz and I was more than happy to do what I was asked to do! Wherever I went making personal appearances, for car shows and other PR events, thousands of people showed up, because of my fame as *Jagger Cates* in *General Hospital.*

I had done all I could to make my role in *General Hospital* a success. Our ratings success was down to the production, the hard work done by the cast I was working with as well as the Executive Producer and all who were in the show, who collectively made it the number two rated show at that time. And for good reason, the hard work and teamwork made it so. The number one show back then was *"The Young and the Restless."*

Steve Burton, Cari Shayne, Vanessa, Marcil and me, all worked non-stop on our story lines long before each scene was filmed. We were dealing with very current subjects like Aids, which at that time was a controversial subject to consider putting into a daily soap.

We had writers to write each story and it was up to them to come up with a general story line. Then the cast in the story all got together to work out how that story would develop and what we each would be saying and how we should be acting in each scene to make it seem real.

During those years, I was becoming a father, a household name and a well-known TV personality all at once and there didn't seem to be enough hours in the day for me then, to do it all.

Maybe *Jagger Cates* will return and who knows what the future holds. That is always the possibility with shows like *General Hospital*, there is always the possibility to go back if the producers think it will gain viewers.

I had bags and bags of fan-mail waiting for me every day I was on the show. In fact, there was so much fan-mail I had an assistant to go through the hundreds of letters I received every day. As a result of playing my part in *General Hospital,* I was travelling all over the US and Canada, opening car shows, doing TV appearances, talk shows and I was a very public and well-known figure.

When I look back at the success of *General Hospital* and the characters we portrayed, I like to think that all our collective work, seen and enjoyed by millions, made our audience's lives a little more fun watching the plots, the characters and the stories that we created unfold on their TVs.

Earth 2

It was 1994 when I decided to leave *General Hospital*, it was because I wanted to do other things, I didn't want to be type-cast as a purely soap star actor. But don't get me wrong here, *General Hospital* was fantastic to work on and I loved all the time I was there and working with the crew and the other actors was a great experience.

My role as *Jagger Cates* brought increased popularity for the show and this was important to me as it showed me that acting with the best of my ability, following the daily coaching and playing my role to the highest standard I could, made a difference.

With what I was doing at *General Hospital* I could have gone for roles in *"Friends"* or *"ER"* as these were also being discussed with me at that time. But I wanted to move into the main-stream movies and not remain too long in soaps.

At this time, I had many choices with shows that wanted me on them, but I had the opportunity to work on a made for TV film, which I hoped would become a series. The show was called *Earth 2,* produced by Steven Spielberg. It had always been my dream to work on a Steven Spielberg project. *Earth 2* was expected to be the biggest Sci Fi show of all time, according to all the pundits. The trailer alone cost ten million dollars! So how could it fail?

They offered me a lead role as *Alonzo Solace* who was the pilot who flew the spaceship, who was able to communicate with the aliens and fly the ship to the new planet, this was a big role for me.

Earth 2 was an American science fiction television series which aired on NBC from November 6, 1994, to June 4, 1995. However, the show was canceled after only one season of 21 episodes. The story follows the journey and settlement of a small expeditionary group called the Eden Project. They were to journey to an Earth-like planet called G889 in an attempt to find a cure to an illness called "the syndrome" The series produced by Amblin Entertainment and Universal Television and was filmed mainly in northern New Mexico around Santa Fe.

In all the movies, shows and professional work I have done, I was professional, which was something my father had instilled in me from a very early age. When I was working on *Earth 2* following *General Hospital,* my character had an on-screen relationship with Jessica Steen, who was a Canadian actress and a wonderful person to work with. We became close friends and I got to know her and her boyfriend, very well, after all when we were filming in New Mexico, we were together for a year, in 1994, filming that show!

Anyway, while we were filming we were working very long hours. At one point, during filming, Jessica was coming down with something and was not feeling well at all, which we could all see. But she was still trying to work and the director just kept her working.

She was feeling worse as the days shoot continued and after seeing how badly the director was treating her, I had to put my foot down and told him, "If you don't take care of Jessica and let her go home to get well, I'm walking!" Sometimes you have to step up and do the right thing whatever the outcome. They gave her the rest she needed and she came back to do what she does best, acting and playing her part right alongside me and now she was back on her game and doing great.

I remembered my father doing that for me, all those years before in Italy, when I was first beginning my career in movies, when he said those same words to the director, over in Italy, because he was mistreating me. It was my chance to do the same now for someone else and I didn't think twice.

When the show was aired, however, it didn't do as well as we all had expected it to do. We hoped it would get a second season where we could take the story further. However, despite being produced by Steven Spielberg, it never made a second season.

Even in movies, like *Earth 2* slated to be big box office or TV hits, there is no certainty as to whether any show will hit the mark. *Earth 2* didn't make it past that first season, so it was time to move on to my next project.

When a film, performance, TV show or even a personal appearance does not meet the audience's expectations, it can ruin a career very quickly. With *Earth 2* we all expected it to become a big success, whereas, in reality, only very few sci-fi movies have ever made the mark to become classics. *2001 A Space Odyssey* led the way and despite the huge amount of money thrown at *Earth 2* it wasn't popular enough to make it past that first season. In hindsight we can always wish we had done something different and the risk for an actor being part of a project that misses the mark, is huge.

But, as they say, "That's Showbusiness!" In conclusion, even working with the very best producers like Steven Spielberg it does not always guarantee a successful movie or show will be made. At the end of the day, it is you the public, who decide whether a show or movie will be a success and money in the production, or even the famous names in that production, may not in the end, make any difference.

Aaron Spelling and *Melrose Place*

After I completed filming *Earth 2*, I received offers for many potential roles in movies and TV shows, in fact it was difficult to choose my next role. Among the many calls I had was one from, none other than Aaron Spelling, inviting me to meet him to discuss a possible role in *Melrose Place*. I flew from New Mexico to LA, after we had completed filming *Earth 2* and went to meet the legendary Aaron Spelling at his offices in Hollywood. He discussed with me the role of Jack Perezi playing opposite Heather Locklear.

I have to admit, meeting the legendary Aaron Spelling, in his huge office, was incredible. We really got along very well and he was easy to talk with as he explained the role he wanted me to play. He was complimentary on my previous work and showed no delusions of grandeur, despite being one of the most successful Hollywood producers ever.

I found him to be a down-to-earth person and you would never imagine you were talking to the most successful producer ever. We both talked about our families and he seemed sincerely interested to learn about my family. I knew that this would be a great company to work with, after meeting Aaron Spelling and learning his philosophy of a happy team makes a good movie. I signed the contract directly with Aaron Spelling and his company Fox.

Aaron Spelling was and still is a legend and had the touch of gold with so many highly successful TV and film shows that had his name associated with his productions. There were over 200 in all and each one was one he had a hand in producing was a success.

For me to be picked by him I knew I had done well and to land a role as requested directly by Aaron Spelling was an accolade for me. All my rehearsing and acting lessons had paid off. I was excited to be working with Heather Locklear (I was a fan) and I was really looking forward to meeting her on the set of *Melrose Place*.

I was in 7 episodes and Heather and I got on very well. I have to say the crew, the director and the entire company were so good to work with, so how could I fail? Heather was always making us laugh and she was delighted to be sharing lines and acting together.

Sometimes that isn't the case and there have been several productions that for me were extremely hard work. But this was not so in working so closely with Heather and the crew.

Heather and I talked a lot between filming and she spoke often of her family and how much they meant to her, which was the same with me. As for her acting, she was a true professional and together we made some great appearances in *Melrose Place*. She was easy to get along with and I have to say that time went by very fast. Before I knew it, it was time to leave the show when my role came to a natural conclusion. The cast and crew gave me a great send-off and I would definitely go back to working there if it was still being filmed, because it was, for me, that good.

However, when it was time to leave I felt it was time to move on to my next project so I wanted to move on to making movies and had decided that although TV shows were great to do, I wanted to be known as a movie actor more than a TV soap actor.

Behind The Scenes

In this business many actors will, when we meet off set, talk mainly about themselves and what they've done. They go to great lengths to tell us what they are working on next, their upcoming projects and all the things centered around themselves and their work. They are the center of their own universe and maybe we all are. They have to believe this in order to deal with the ups and downs of their professional life, which believe me are full of extreme highs and lows!

However, that wasn't me, I always preferred to listen more than I talked (another lesson from my dad). Of course, if people asked me about certain things I had done and if asked I would tell them, but for me when we were working together, that's what was important to me. I felt I always had to remain professional and help those I worked with whenever I could.

I'm not an extrovert and I like to think that those who have worked with me see me the same way, but you'll have to ask them about that. I became a good listener and companion to all who I worked with, the cast, the crew, all of them because to me they were all equally important in making the show a success. After all, it was up to all of us to make it so.

If any of the women I worked with, were ever asked, what they thought it was like working with me, I hope they would say, I was a person who was always professional to work with.

I never slept with any of the female actresses, I was working with, ever. In fact, on many of the shows I was working on, people I was working with could do as they wished with whoever, as they say, what happens on the road, stays on the road. But not for me, I was not and am not that person at all.

Padre Papa

In 1996, when I was doing, *"Padre Papa,"* I was playing Don Giuseppe, an American priest. It was an Italian mini-series and was a big hit in Italy. That show was on for an hour and a half every night. It was a very interesting project because all my lines were in English, even though it was an Italian show. I was working with the actress, Maria Grazia Cucinotta, who was considered one of the most beautiful women in the world having that beautiful dark Mediterranean look. Maria was from Sicily, in fact not far from where my father was from.

Maria was five feet ten tall and was in the James Bond movie, *"The World Is Not Enough,"* where she played "The Cigar Girl." She, like me, was also a well-known model and went on to become a producer and director. To me, she was right up there with Monica Bellucci as a beautiful actress and top model. We became like brother and sister, in fact it was like working with my sister, Simonne, and we became great friends.

The funny thing about making that movie was that I was acting in English, Maria was acting in Italian and then everybody else was acting in German! The entire movie was filmed in three languages.

I could speak English and Italian fluently and while Maria spoke Italian and maybe a little English, everyone else spoke German. So, we had to work together learning what the last word was, from any of the lines that were spoken in German, which we didn't understand, to know when our lines were to be spoken next.

It was so funny, but we got used to it. Can you imagine, having a conversation that you have to make seem real, being filmed, while not understanding what the hell is being said yet answering it as if you did understand and all in a three-language conversation! If you get the chance, look up the movie *"Papa Padre"* and you'll see what I mean.

Making a great movie is challenging as there are so many changes along the way, changes in scenes, in scripts, in the lines, the lighting in fact every little detail and that is why a good Director is so controlling. He or she has to be, to keep an eye on the plot and imagine how each and every detail will look when it's all put together.

The scenes that are filmed are seldom in sequence, so the director and the editors have to keep focused on each component, continuity, plot, lighting, making every movie a work of art. Believe me, if in one shot there is a cup in one position on a table, it had better still be there in all other shots otherwise people who love to find mistakes, will certainly voice their findings loud and clear that continuity sucks!

That's why not many actors can transition into becoming a director. It is a skill quite different from acting, with an unbelievably detailed mindset. The director is the one person who can visualize how each scene fits together to create the finished movie.

Even though I was working so much and on so many plots and storylines, I was never satisfied with what I was doing. I always hoped my next movie would be "That special one," the one people would remember me by. But in each and every movie, I gave it my best, something my father had said many, many times as he drilled this truth into me. As any actor will tell you, you have to play your part the very best you can, to perfection, according to each director and script writer, so every film you make has the very best chance to be a success. I love it!

A good actor makes any part believable no matter the language.

Chapter 32

Virginia Madsen

Around the time I was *filming General Hospital*, I had started a relationship with Virginia Madsen. Virginia had been married to actor and director Danny Huston, John Huston's son, after they had met on the set of *Mr. North*. They divorced in 1992 before Virginia and I met. I was always attracted to Virginia but at the same time I of course respect marriage so we only began to date after her own marriage was over.

How Virginia and I met was because close to where my mother lived was a restaurant with a pool bar called "Trinity" which was a well-known hang out, not far from Marina Del Rey where I lived. A number of celebrities and I went there and I got to know the bartender quite well. This was before I started work on *General Hospital*. Virginia used to come in with Danny Huston, so we met each other there quite often and chatted as friends.

They invited me to their home several times and we got to know each other while becoming good friends. She threw many parties and I was often invited to them. She was always making sure everything was perfect, the food, the drinks, the people she invited and she took time to be the perfect host, something she was very good at. Her parties were always successful with a lot of actors and film people who went to them and although I recognized many of them, I could never remember all the work they had done.

After her divorce from Danny, we met again at a music awards show, Madonna was there along with many other big names as well. Virginia was seated next to another mutual girlfriend who had her own jewelry line. When we saw each other that time we just clicked from the get-go. We both exchanged numbers that night and sometime later a friend called me, telling me Virginia was asking after me and suggested I call her. I called her and we began a great relationship where we eventually both fell in love.

In summer 1993 we went on vacation together to Mexico it was the perfect vacation and we had a wonderful time there. One night we both wanted to go out for a drink, but the closest bar was quite a distance away. It was pitch black that night and we had to walk along a very narrow path that we couldn't see very clearly. We walked along the long path to the bar, but Virginia had weak ankles, following an accident she had in a movie she was in sometime before.

Anyway, on our way back home from the bar, while walking down the same dark path we had walked on earlier, she stepped into a hole and hurt her ankle. We didn't know how badly she had damaged it at the time, but she was in a lot of pain, so I picked her up and carried her for two miles back to the hotel. I was wearing flip flops and as you can imagine the walk was quite difficult.

When we finally got to our hotel, her ankle had swollen up badly and she was in a lot of pain. The hotel called a local doctor and one arrived shortly after, but he didn't know what he was doing. All he did was to put some cream on her now very swollen ankle, I was thinking "cream" really?" The following morning her ankle, not surprisingly, was now worse so we decided to go to a hospital in Cancun and I rented a car to drive us there.

As luck would have it, on the way to the hospital, we had a flat tire! I pulled over to change the tire and after it was fixed, we drove on to the hospital. They took an x-ray of her ankle and told us it was a bad sprain. They placed her in an ankle-brace and told her she had to rest it.

After we came back home, we started to have arguments and that led to us having a huge verbal disagreement. As a result, what was to be a perfect vacation ended up with us splitting up, it was awful for us both as we both went our separate ways. I felt terrible about how we had parted, so I wrote many letters of apology to her. I explained that it was entirely my fault, which I knew it was, I had gotten mad and I was the cause of our argument.

Several months later, Virginia called me out of the blue to say she had some news to tell me and asked me to come to her house. At the time I was living in an apartment, overlooking the marina, in Marina Del Rey.

I drove to her house and after some small talk with me asking her how she had been and what she was doing, she told me she had some news to tell me. I had no idea what it was, so I sat quietly waiting for her news. She found out her foot was in fact broken but was now on the mend and she was in a cast. Then she told me she was pregnant!

She had told me before, when we were dating, that she could never get pregnant and I understood this to be the case, but it made no difference to us. She had been told this several years before. So now she was in fact pregnant with what seemed a miracle baby! It was during the vacation in Cancun probably before she broke her foot, that we believed our son Jack was conceived. That was in August and this was now October when we met again for her to tell me her news.

After she told me she was pregnant we got back together again and I put many things I had going at the time on hold as I wanted to be with her and to be a father. Family to me was and always will be everything!

When we were getting back together, Virginia was about to file bankruptcy because her career had not been doing well at all. Perhaps also like me, she had made some decisions that did not work out as expected, in choosing to make some movies that were not very successful. Like me, she didn't know that at the time as none of us do when we sign a movie contract if the movie will be a success. These are mistakes we can all make, in the movie industry and I've made those mistakes too. Anyway, very soon we became a couple again.

Virginia gave birth to our son Jack, who was born in Cedar Sinai Hospital in LA. on August 6th in the summer of 1994. At that time, I was working on *Earth 2* down in Santa Fe, New Mexico. She brought our baby, Jack, down to New Mexico and we lived there together for a year, while I was filming *Earth 2*. We had a great time being together with our new baby. I was so happy then and I took good care of her, doing all I could to look after her and our baby, Jack, when I was not filming.

That TV show, *Earth 2,* didn't do as well as we all hoped it would. The show was eventually cancelled, before we started filming season two, because it was too expensive and had not made the revenue they hoped it would. We were told that was the reason, but whatever the reason, it was not to be picked up for a second season. When we knew *Earth 2* was not going to go forward. Virginia went back to her career taking our son, baby Jack, with her. Later we shared looking after Jack each doing our part.

When I think honestly about our time together, I wanted to be more of a family man, at that time, while Virginia wanted her career to move forward and get back on track so she moved ahead with her career, a natural conclusion with both of us wanting to focus on different futures.

Looking back, now and being completely honest, which is what my book is about, at that time we both wanted different things from life. Had we talked openly and honestly at the time, I would have tried to convince her to stay together for Jack's sake, who we both loved very much.

But at the end of the day, to convince a partner to stay together when one partner wants to leave the relationship, will never work. We split up after a three-year relationship. Jack went to live with Virginia, in Hollywood, but spent almost equal time with me. Sadly, we both went our separate ways.

Many years later, Virginia and I ended up living across the road from each other in "Thousand Oaks" in Ventura County California for a long while. She was now part of the Film Academy and was able to vote several celebrities in, as well as voting for her choice for Academy Award winners.

I had always wanted to be a part of the prestigious Academy Awards and I hoped, since Virginia was a member in the academy and had been nominated for awards by them, that she might be able to help me to join.

But the academy said no to my requests and wouldn't even consider taking my petition that I sent them despite all the work I had done in movies, here in the US and in Italy; my TV shows and the reality shows were now totaling more than 90 appearances when I tried to join. But we seldom get what we want.

Virginia did very well, as Maya in **Alexander Payne's film,** *Sideways* **(2004), for** which she received nominations for a Golden Globe and an Academy award for Best Supporting Actress. Her career picked back up and as she is an outstanding actress I wasn't surprised.

Life is short and trying to make a relationship work when both sides want different things from life is a waste of time.

Chapter 33

Tom Cruise

My favorite actor was always Tom Cruise. To me he represented all I wanted to be. I watched all of the Tom Cruise movies and when I first came over from Italy, he was like a big brother to me though he would never know this. Not in any real sense, of course, but as I was a private and shy boy of thirteen, I imagined doing the same things he did in his movies. I loved seeing his work and I watched him and studied his acting. I saw his many films over and over again seeing how he moved in the many stunts he did.

I finally got to meet him for the first time, in 1996, at the premier of *"Mission Impossible."* My sister **Simonne** was with me at the time. I also met Shirley McLaine there, but for me, meeting Tom was really special. I was impressed with what I saw. Tom was humble, quiet, cordial and not at all how I thought he might be. We just made small talk then as he was very busy being at the premier of the movie, he was starring in he had to leave us.

No one knew Tom Cruise was my idol or that I was learning from all I saw him in. This was private to me and me only at that time. But we shared an interest in many things we loved, mainly racing cars and action parts in movies.

I met Tom a second time four years later, in 2000, for the premier of *Mission Impossible 2*, once again he was quiet and hardly spoke. For me though, it was quite surreal. I have met many big stars, as you can see from my photos and had great conversations with them all, but Tom was not the same, he was quite laid back. A photo was taken then which I treasure. I have kept it, as it was a special day for me in meeting him and now I've included it here in my book.

I was thinking, just recently, wouldn't it be great if the one person I respected the most, Tom Cruise, was the one to bring me back to acting again in movies.

We live and dream!

Chapter 34

Big Bobby

Big Bobby was one of my closest and oldest friends, we were like brothers. I was doing a movie called *"Fatal Error,"* in 1999, I starred with Janine Turner and the movie was directed by a friend of mine, Armand Mastroianni. I was playing Dr. Nick Baldwin in the movie, Nick was an EMT emergency driver. The role I was playing was that guy who arrives on the scene when an emergency has just happened and knows exactly what to do when all hell is letting loose.

I liked the role I was playing, going out in ambulances, making quick, life-saving decisions and all that went along with my role. I imagined what it would be like to be a real first responder actually saving lives for a living.

I went to New York, with my sister Simonne, to promote the movie and a good friend of mine Robert DiAngelo, who was always "Big Bobby," to me. He was going to meet me there and we were going to hang out for the evening together and to catch up with what we were both doing at the time. Big Bobby was, to me, like a large version of Robert De Niro. He was bigger but he had the same vibe.

Anyway, we agreed to meet at The Four Seasons Hotel where I was staying. Bobby wanted to hear all about my son, my family and everything I had been doing with my career. I was looking forward to meeting my old friend as we had done everything together in the past.

Big Bobby wanted to take me out to the clubs that evening, but I didn't want to do that as I had a very early call to go on the *Rosie O'Donnell show*, the following morning. All I wanted to do was to go to a restaurant and catch up, as I wanted to be on my game early, to get ready for my interview with Rosie.

Anyway, Bobby insisted so I asked Simonne if she would like to join us. She said no reminding me we had an early call the next day. Bobby took me to a club called *The China Club* in downtown New York where he was well known.

I didn't really want to go but we went anyway because I really loved Bobby. I had missed our time together and looked at spending as much time as I could with my friend Big Bobby so the venue didn't really matter.

It was a Monday night when we were in the VIP room and the club was packed that night. I went to the bar to get a drink, but I was only drinking orange juice. I wasn't a drinker anyway and never had been and I always liked drinking orange juice when I went out.

While I was at the bar, I looked over and saw that Bobby was having an altercation with another man. Apparently two girls were drinking at Bobby's table and one got up, drunk, falling onto the table. Bobby and a man sitting at that table, started to have words.

Anyway, Bobby and this other dude, were now standing, going at it back and forth, arguing and they were getting louder. I knew there was going to be a fight. I always watch my back, but as I went over to Bobby, the other guy had already left before I got to them.

Bobby started to walk away from me before I got there, so I asked him, "Hey Bobby what's up." But he was now leaning on me, as we walked out of the club and I had no idea he was badly hurt.

He slumped over me, so I picked him up, he was well over two hundred and fifty pounds and he was not easy to pick up or support. I was trying to take him all the way down the stairs, to take him out of the club, but he was getting weaker as we descended the stairs.

I looked at my friend in shock as his face was now ashen, "I got stabbed!" he whispered as he began to slouch over and as I looked down, I saw blood everywhere coming from his stomach. I was pushing his bad stomach wound in my hands trying to stop the bleeding as his guts were now coming out over my hands. It was not sinking in as to what had just occurred.

We finally made it, stumbling down the stairs to the street, but Bobby couldn't now stand up so I laid him down on the pavement. It felt like a scene from a movie and was surreal to me, but unlike the movie I was doing at the time, this was real life and he was getting worse before my eyes. I was very scared for my friend thinking he might actually die right here on the street. I had my hand on his wound and I was pressing it to keep his guts from spilling out onto the pavement and to stem the bleeding.

There was no one around on that street and I was screaming out as loud as I could to the empty street, "Someone call an ambulance, call the police!" My eyes were all red and I looked like a demon as I was trying to get my friend some help while cradling his slumped head in my arms.

The ambulance took what seemed to be a lifetime to arrive and I was trying to keep Bobby alive the whole time telling him to stay with me, stay with me.

Bobby was having none of this and was shouting," I'm gonna get that dude and when I do, I'm gonna kill him!" He was having a panic attack and the adrenaline was kicking in. He was going into a traumatic shock. I was to find out later, the stabbing had damaged his spleen and he was in a really bad way.

Finally, the ambulance came and these two EMT's were the guys I had been playing in my movie right at the same time as this all went down. They tried to tell me I was not allowed in the ambulance, but I told them, "You're gonna have to kill me first I'm going with him and there's nothing you can do to stop me!"

I jumped straight into the ambulance and stayed with him all the way to the hospital, holding his hand all the way there. He went straight into surgery where they worked on him and managed to keep him alive. It was now two or three in the morning when I called his parents to tell them what had happened. I had known them for years; they were good people and were like family to me.

Then the detectives arrived at the hospital, shortly after Bobby went into the OR and there seemed to be a crowd of people gathered around me. Everyone was asking the same thing, "What happened, what happened?"

That morning it was all over the news, saying "Antonio Sabato Jr. was involved in a stabbing in a New York club!" Perfect! My mom and dad were frantically calling me asking if I was ok and wanting to know what was going on and what happened. They were worried sick.

My sister woke up to the news on the TV in her hotel room and was also calling me wanting to know what happened. I was coming back from the hospital and I hadn't even managed to get changed for my appearance on Rosie O'Donnell's show, because I had been up all night talking to the detectives explaining what had happened. My clothes were blood stained and I looked and felt a real mess.

I rushed to my room to get myself as ready as I could for the Rosie McDonald show that same morning. While I was on her show, I was so wound up with all that had happened that my energy level was very low. Rosie had been told what had happened and asked me about it, so I told her exactly what had occurred at *The China Club* the previous night, partly to stop the speculation that was gathering speed in the media.

Later that morning, I called Bobby, he was now all stitched up, but he was still very angry at what had happened. He was telling me he wanted to go back to the club and, "find that dude" to kill him! I kept telling him, "Bobby forget it, what's happened has happened, forget it." But he was inconsolable and was getting more and more angry working himself up.

I told Bobby that the following day I had to fly to Italy to do a movie, but I would call him every day while I was there. The movie was *"Vola Sciusciù."* and was an Italian film. I was playing an American Soldier; it was a made for TV drama and I would be away for some time.

Before I left New York, for Italy, I visited Bobby and I told him that when I got back, I would come to New York, pick him up and he could hang out with me in California. He loved the idea and it was a possibility for us to spend more time together.

But Bobby was still growing more upset now and was becoming inconsolable, working himself up more and more, saying he was angry at having terrible scars on his stomach. He told me he would never be able to go to the beach now. Apparently, the internal damage was extremely bad following his stabbing and they had to go in to do internal stitches. It was not just a stabbing it was a slashing as well.

I flew to Italy where we were filming on the other side of the Adriatic Sea. I would be very far away and on a different time zone, but as promised, I called Bobby at the hospital every day. After only a few days, the nurses stopped telling me anything and it all went silent for me. I called Bobby's mom and she always returned my calls, but this time she didn't return my calls either.

I then called around to find someone who could tell me what the hell was going on. Later, a good friend of mine, George Alvarez, told me my friend Bobby had died in hospital. I was stunned and very upset. Apparently, Bobby in his continuing and worsening anger, had opened up his internal stitches so he had to go back into surgery for the internal wounds to be closed again.

He was then placed into an induced coma to help his body to heal and to prevent him from becoming angry again at what had happened to him, at the club, in a place where he had many friends.

Sadly, his situation deteriorated to such an extent, after that second surgery, that his mother had to pull the plug as he was becoming worse by the hour and was beyond any help the hospital could give him. While he was in his coma, he died, in that same hospital I had taken him to. I was devastated.

I know I did all I could to save him, but these things were going around and round in my head, what if I been there with him at that table, maybe my friend would still be alive, who knows. It took me a long time to get over my friend Bobby, passing away like that, when we were so looking forward to seeing each other after such a long break. I will always remember my big lovable bear of a friend.

On my return from Italy, I went to see his wife and his family, after his untimely death, to share my condolences. They were all great people who I had known for years and I will keep them as friends always.

When something like this happens, we go over and over in our minds as I did then; what if? What if we had gone to dinner instead, what if I had stayed at the hospital what if, what if. In the end fate plays its hand and there's nothing we can do. My friend Bobby died in May 1999. I still think of him and see him clearly in my mind.

I miss you my great big-hearted friend, Robert DiAngelo, my "Big Bobby." Rest in Peace, my beautiful friend and I will always remember you, I promise you that.

More Bobby's

Sometime later, I was down in Australia doing a TV mini-series called *"Tribe"* playing the part of *Jack Osborn.* The film was an action/adventure mini-series. Starring Craig McLachlan, Nadine Garner, Rachel Blakely and Joanna Cassidy. We were filming in Queensland Australia.

While I was there, I met two really great guys, who were both called Robert or "Bobby". While I was on the set, the director, George Miller, called me an "honorable man" which after all I had been through, was uplifting for me to hear. It was an outward sign that I was being the person I wanted to be my new self. Even now I smile at his comment to me, just when I needed to hear it. It was like a message to me from God Himself, telling me I was now getting back on track.

Anyway, my two friends, Robert and Robert, lived in Melbourne, Australia, one is an actor while the other owns several gas stations, one being Italian while the other is Lebanese. Bobby and Bobby are two wonderful guys and to this day we remain close friends. The more I thought about them both and me meeting them both so soon after my friend "Big Bobby" had died, the more I thought, I lost one Bobby and got two back! They helped me to get over my loss and we remain friends still.

They say, "Time Heals," but the hole left in our lives, when a close friend dies unexpectedly, is always there.

Chapter 35

<hr>

No Excuses

<hr>

While I was filming in so many different locations, I made sure I always found a local Gym to continue working out. This was especially important for me since maintaining my body was important for the parts and appearances I made. It didn't matter where I was and wherever possible I checked out any local gyms in advance. I would call ahead to find out information on all the local gyms before I even arrived at the film location. When I found a gym, I called and asked them who the master trainer or "Dojo' was and I would talk to the Sensei to find out what his personal methods and skills were and how he worked. I then set up a session with them to see what I could learn from them.

I asked if I could work out with him or her and once again, I was watching and learning all I could from their techniques to see what I could add to my own routines. It didn't matter where I was, I had to be there as often as I could while I was on location. It didn't matter either if the trainer was male of female they were equally as good from my experience.

I took a little from each of the many trainers I came across and built up my knowledge of how to train and how to maintain my body shape without expensive training equipment, which would have been impossible to drag around with me on the many locations I filmed at.

I was also gaining experience from the best, from watching old fitness movies showing the methods people like Bruce Lee or Sugar Ray. Keeping my body in perfect shape was as and still is a way of life for me. All the different training methods I had used, I memorized, together with the many training videos I bought.

This led me to begin to invent my own training routines working on development of specific muscle groups to develop the body shape I wanted. It was also important that I kept my workouts balanced so my body didn't have any increased muscle mass in one specific area of my body and even more important was that I didn't want to look like an over muscled body builder.

Gary Leonard and Mohammed Ali had adopted great methods to keep their bodies in perfect shape. I had watched their style in videos as I was building up my knowledge and the methods I would use so I started using them in my training routines.

If filming was early in the morning I would go to the gym late, if filming was starting later, because of a camera set up or particular lighting conditions, or weather-related issues, I would work out early before filming began.

I decided to write down everything I had learned into a book called *"No Excuses."* It took a lot of effort to get the book written how I wanted it, so that others could learn from my book and do the exercise routines that I had laid out and in such a way that worked for them.

My book sold 300,000 copies and I was very happy, not just for the number of books that were sold, but the reputation my book was gaining along with the successes I was hearing about from the people who bought it.

I did many interviews and appearances, on TV, in radio shows and in magazines telling people about my work-out and exercise routines and I was an example of how these routines could help others to stay in shape, no matter what job they had or what their lifestyle was.

I received fan mail from everywhere and people were telling me how my book had changed their lives. This made me happy to see how much I had helped others now, not only making my fans happy with the films I was in but on a more personal level in helping them to be happy with how they looked and felt about themselves.

I'll be bringing out another work-out and lifestyle change book with much more about how to say in shape as an older person, which I think people of an older age would like to read. I am now in my 50s and I am training harder than ever twice a day 7 days a week and training for professional motor racing and looking my very best.

Keeping myself in top form is a way of life for me and I will never change this.

Chapter 36

Why I Train

At the **age** of 51, approaching the milestone of 52, I have embarked on a rigorous physical training routine like never before. Motivated by my passion for motor racing, I have committed myself to a grueling regimen that involves training twice a day, seven days a week. This chapter delves into my training journey, highlighting the dedication, discipline and lifestyle changes that have become integral to my pursuit of excellence.

Setting the Stage: Before diving into the details of my training routine, it is essential to understand the mindset and motivation behind my decision to do a more strenuous workout routine. Motor racing is an adrenaline-fueled sport and, as you now understand, has always held a special place in my heart. With a desire to compete at the highest level, I realized that physical fitness would be the key to unlocking my potential on the track. Thus, I embarked on a journey to transform my body and elevate my performance.

My Training Regimen: My training regimen is characterized by its intensity and consistency. Twice a day, every day, I push my body to its limits through a combination of cardiovascular exercises and weight training. The mornings are dedicated to cardiovascular workouts, which include activities like running, cycling, or swimming. These exercises not only improve my endurance but also enhance my cardiovascular health, ensuring that I can sustain the high-speed demands and quick decision making of motor racing.

The afternoons are reserved for weight training, where I focus on building strength and muscle. This routine includes a variety of exercises targeting different muscle groups, allowing me to develop a well-rounded physique. By incorporating weight training into my regimen, I aim to enhance my overall performance, as strength plays a crucial role in maneuvering the race car and withstanding the physical demands of the sport.

Diet and Nutrition: Diet and Nutrition complements my intense training routine is a carefully curated diet plan. Recognizing the importance of fueling my body with the right nutrients, I have adopted a lifestyle of conscious eating. I follow a two-meal-a-day schedule, with my first meal at noon and the second meal before dinner, typically between 6:30 PM and 7:30 PM. This approach allows me to maintain a high protein, low carbohydrate diet, providing the necessary energy for my training sessions while promoting muscle growth and fast recovery.

The Precision Lifestyle: To achieve my optimal results, meant I have embraced a lifestyle of precision and discipline. Every aspect of my routine, from training to nutrition, is meticulously planned and executed. I prioritize rest and recovery, ensuring that my body has ample time to heal and rejuvenate.

Sleep is a crucial component of this lifestyle, as it allows my body to recover and adapt to the physical stress imposed during training.

Challenges and Rewards: Undertaking such an intensive training regimen at the age of 51 does not come without its challenges. There are days when fatigue sets in and the motivation to continue wavers. However, it is during these moments that I remind myself of my ultimate goal, which is to excel in motor racing. The rewards of my training journey, both physical and mental, keep me focused and determined. Increased strength, improved endurance, and a sense of accomplishment serve as constant reminders of the progress made and the potential yet to be unlocked.

Conclusion: In conclusion, my training journey at the age of 51 has been nothing short of transformative. Through a combination of intense physical training, a disciplined diet, and a precision lifestyle, I have pushed my limits and redefined what, for me, is possible. As I approach my 52nd birthday, I am filled with excitement and anticipation for the challenges and victories that lie ahead. This journey has taught me that age is just a number, and with dedication and perseverance, one can achieve greatness at any stage of life.

Keeping fit and taking good care of my body is a way of life for me.

Some of my modeling and body Form photos

As Photographed

by

Jason Ellis Photography.

@Jasonellisphotography.com

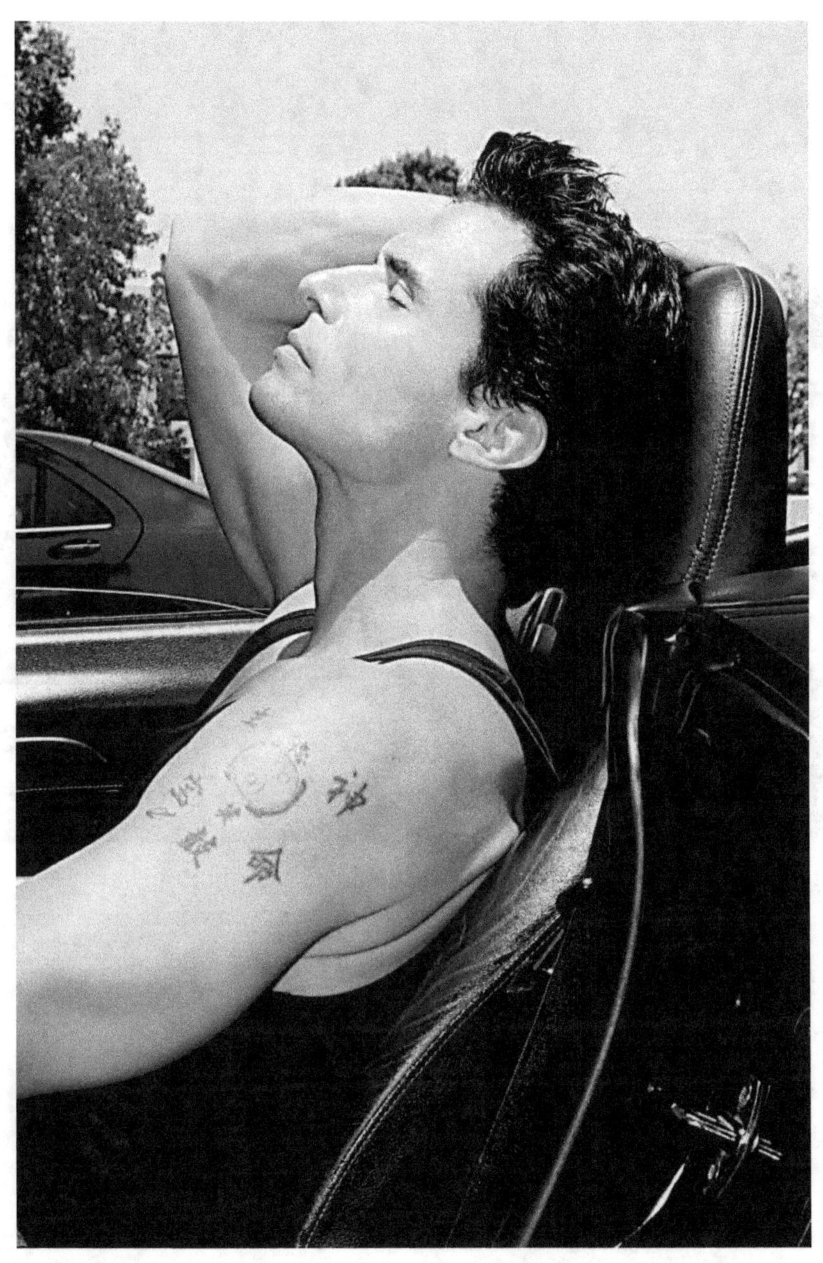

Being prepared for a photo shoot with my
daughter Mina looking on.

With my daughter Mina

216

Chapter 37

My Battle with Addiction

Before witnessing firsthand, the events that led to Bobby's death, the only other time I had ever experienced death first-hand, was while we were living in Italy, my paternal grandmother who I loved very much, died. Her name was Agatha Sabato and she died in 1983, before we moved to the U.S.

I was a young boy then, but after she died, I went into my room and turned all the lights off and laid on my bed not wanting to be with anyone at all. She was the person who kept the family together. I remember hiding behind the curtains and bawling my eyes out because I was so sad at losing my grandmother. It was the first personal loss I had ever experienced.

Now, right after Bobby's death, in 1999, I went on a rampage, I crashed my "Ferrari Maranello 550," at 160 miles per hour when I drove it into a wall at Marina Del Rey at 2am in the morning. I was driving too fast when I felt the back end begin to slip. The front end started to feel loose too. I knew how to drive but I was going way too fast for the road I was on.

My car caught fire in the crash and I was lucky to get out alive. My Ferrari's V12 engine had saved my life by taking the explosive impact. I did all the things I could to destroy my life back then and I didn't care. Looking back if it had been another car like a Porsche with a mid-engine or a rear engine, I would be dead. I am convinced God played a hand in saving my life. Instead, I had bruises all over me, but no real damage, I was lucky then, but later when the pain came it was unbearably bad.

Even as a young boy while we were living in Rome, I always hung out with older boys. Many of them were smoking and using "Hash," I tried it too, mainly to "fit in" with the crowd, but I was never addicted and could take it or leave it and I have to be honest I hated it!

Then in my twenties, I thought I would always be the one in charge of me, that I would never become addicted. I was eating healthily and had been working-out all throughout my life. I thought I was different from the people I knew who were addicted to drugs. Back then I thought I could handle it, recreationally, but I was surrounded by people, friends and acquaintances at the time, who were all doing drugs. So, I convinced myself it was probably OK, but it was not OK!

Following that car crash I was in tremendous pain from all the bruising all over my body. I was fighting a war on two fronts, my pain and the loss of my closest friend. I tried smoking weed but that led me to trying other drugs including Crystal Meth, which was cheap and it was highly addictive. But I believed that I could handle it just like so many others who were in the same position and I would not become addicted.

My vision of an addict, back then, was someone, like those I had seen in Rome, sitting on the side of the street spaced out and filthy dirty. I did not see myself as looking at all like that. Anyway, of course I was totally wrong! I was just like so many others the same as me, trying to deal with addiction, thinking and fooling myself, that I could still handle it. I was taking Crystal Meth and I was going downhill. It happened so gradually I hardly noticed it.

I eventually came to the realization I had to deal with this and deal with it very quickly. I eventually managed to get out of this addiction which was very hard to do but I was determined to beat it and I did manage to quit.

As I was getting through this, my doctor told me, I couldn't simply stay clean cold turkey and I needed to be on another medication to help me "level out" as he put it. I managed to get free of my one addiction and I was finally clean but with the help of my doctor's "levelling out meds." I began to rely on what he had prescribed.

However, after being completely clean for fifteen years, I was now becoming addicted to prescription meds and I was "climbing back on the horse." Cheryl was my wife at that time and she had no idea about my addiction at all because I showed no outward signs of my growing addiction to the prescribed pain meds. I had moved on to prescription sleeping pills which were prescribed for me. Cheryl still had no idea I was using prescription medications until I told her about it and that was long after I had started. There were no signs that she ever saw of my prescription drug use. But I think it was probably her aggressive lawyers, coupled with her anger at me, who made that story up as we both knew I had completed the rehab.

In 2016 My relationship with Cheryl was, not surprisingly, beginning to fall apart as it had seemingly from the very beginning. I think we both knew we should not have gotten married but we did. Cheryl and I both loved our son and he was the reason we had remained together. Although we were staying together for our son, neither of us were right for each other at that time and the rift between us was getting wider. My use of prescription drugs was certainly not helping our relationship. We both loved and cared for our son and we cared for each other, but that wasn't the same as being in love with each other.

I was becoming more and more depressed, so much so that when I went to see my doctor, he put me on anti-depressants, to help with my depression. I think part of my problem was because of my relationship at home and my life at the time. What I was being given was not good for me at all, but at that time I believed in my doctor. We now know that certain pain meds and anti-depressant or sleeping drugs are highly addictive, but back then I was not aware and after all, I trusted my doctor as we all did.

I was worried all the time about what I was going to do about my relationship with Cheryl, which was falling apart around me. I worried too about my next job, whether I would be able to have another acting role, or if I would have money to look after my family and it was all I could think about. I was overwhelmed with the effects of what my addiction was doing to me and I was becoming more depressed with everything. Addiction makes people paranoid and the thoughts keep circling round and around with seemingly no way out.

This is what addiction does, we know we must change and get free of our drug use but doing it is extremely hard. So, when we keep thinking about changing which we haven't done yet, we become more and more depressed with ourselves for failing in this one action. It's a never-ending circle of depression and I was right down in the middle of it.

I stayed awake most of those nights worrying, unable to sleep and little did I know that I was now fully addicted to these prescription meds. I was still doing my workout routines, eating healthy foods, staying in shape, but nevertheless, I was addicted to what I was taking.

One day as I was right in the middle of my addiction, I didn't feel right, something was very wrong, I was continually feeling like I was not on my game, not in control of me and eventually my doctor stopped prescribing the sleeping pills.

That first night when I didn't have any more sleeping pills, I felt was dying! I had never experienced this before and it was, for me, a terrible experience. I was experiencing the craving, the cramps, the withdrawal symptoms but I didn't know it, neither did Cheryl we were completely unaware of what was happening to me.

My Journey into Rehab

I was at the lowest point I had ever been and I hated it. I hated myself and what I was doing. I was looking for someone else to blame but there was no one, this was down to me and I had to deal with it myself.

I didn't want to look at myself in the mirror because I didn't like what I saw. I was at the lowest point I had ever been in my entire life at that time. The cravings were intense but no matter what I tried; I could not control them. I can honestly say I was very scared for who I was at that point and I knew I couldn't get out of this by myself, I needed help.

My whole body was racked in pain with the cravings because my doctor had taken me off the prescription meds cold turkey! I realized I had to do something, I was still forcing myself to work out, every single day and working out was a lifestyle for me regardless of anything else going on in my life at the time. I was keeping myself fit and trying desperately to keep myself "on my game," or trying to, in maintaining my tip top shape as I had always had, or so I convinced myself to believe.

When we are at this point with our addiction as I was then, it takes time to realize what our options are. No one can beat addiction with just their willpower, it's almost impossible. I knew I needed help and I needed it now! So, I called my mom to come and pick me up to take me away to an institution or rehab facility, right then and right there!

She came immediately and booked me in to rehab. When I arrived, I was a mess and needed help just to breathe.

I can honestly say that in hindsight it was the best and the worst experience of my life being in Rehab. I re-learned who I was and I was beginning to find things out about myself that I had never thought about before and I didn't like some of the things I was learning about myself.

People I met there were facing the same problems as me, we were helping each other. We found out we needed a lot of help from each other to deal with the devastation to each of us that was caused by our addiction. My addiction was from prescription meds before the State of Ohio caught on and sued 5 big pharma companies that were selling these highly addictive drugs and my use of them was killing me.

I was hurting everyone around me who saw what these drugs were doing. I can tell you all, people on drugs need all the help they can get as it is so very hard to become clean. As I found out in rehab, some people are pre-wired and have an addictive "gene." It doesn't mean everyone who has this "gene" will become addicted, but once it is triggered a process inside the brain begins to be set in motion. The use of whatever it is that" triggers" your addiction starts to re-wire your brain and it forces you to focus only on "feeding the addiction," over and above and despite everything else.

Addiction even affects eating, where we don't care if we eat or not as long as we feed our addiction. The brain becomes re-wired, so we do not think the same anymore, we get sucked in, feeding the addiction monster. How it affected me was that what I thought was a normal reaction to things going on around me, was not normal at all and I was always thinking about how long it would be to get my next prescription for the painkillers I was now addicted to.

My friends and my family all saw what was happening to me but was too far into my addiction to see it for myself, I thought I could handle this. I still thought I was in control, but I wasn't at all and I reached a decision point where I began to see that if I carried on, I would die.

This is how addiction works and people, around you, think you should simply "choose" to get off drugs, the phrase, "Just say no!" bears no resemblance to the truth behind what addiction really is. If it was just a choice to say that one word, no, then no one would be addicted. But when the brain is re-wired an addict is not aware of the possibility to get off drugs it is extremely difficult.

For me it was a desperately lonely place, a place that I wanted to hide from everyone who knew me and I was spiraling down and out of control. But, at the same time, I was fooling myself because I was working out every day and, so I thought, I was ok. What I didn't realize was that although my body was looking OK my mind was not.

It annoys me still when I hear people saying, "they should just make the choice, choose not to use drugs!" At the back of an addicts mind he or she already knows this but when the brain itself is rewired its extremely hard, if not impossible, to make that to stop choice because your brain is only making you feed its addiction. I was using extraordinarily strong pain killers, but to me and from where I was at the time, I had to do whatever it took to feed my addiction.

I needed to make a change, I needed to believe in a higher power and to ask God to help me. I have always believed in Jesus Christ ever since birth and without that belief, in God, I could never have gotten away from my addiction.

I prayed to God, every single day and sometimes several time each day, to help take this burden from me. But at the end of the day, praying alone was not going to work without a strong and personal desire to get free from drugs. A belief in the higher power that God gives us to heal us for free is what is needed to get free from this evil.

After Bobby died, I was alone with my thoughts, I was busy working but deep inside I felt alone, suffering from acute depression. I was having difficulty dealing with my personal grief but let's be clear, I'm not using my friend's death in any way as an excuse. However, the way Bobby died brought me to a lonely place, a place I couldn't handle. Although, of late Bobby and I had led our own separate lives, at the back of my mind Bobby was always there as is always the case with close friends. We don't always need to be in close proximity but knowing our friends are there is what true friendship is about.

The suddenness of Bobby's death, while we were both out together after such a long time, was a stark reality against all I had experienced before. I now realized death can come calling at any time and I thought I could handle it as part of my daily routine. I was strong, I played strong parts in movies, I worked out and I had a body many people envied. But this was surface level only and underneath all this, I was now lonely and depressed, a close friend had been killed, murdered right in front of me for no reason.

Prescription drugs seemed to help for a short while each time I took them. I was trading off one kind of despair for another and through both I was the loser. My belief in God and in Jesus Christ, was a major part of my upbringing and without that long held belief I can honestly say, I could never ever have gotten out of my addiction with drugs.

Looking back, it was the best and the worst time for me as my time in rehab made me look deeply into myself and I didn't like what I saw. They say when we look into the chasm the chasm stares right back. It certainly looked back at me and deep into my soul. I believed I was always in control and able to handle anything. I was now out of control and by my own doing, no one else was to blame but me. Coming out of this has made me a better person, a person who has stared death in the face and I truly hope those I inadvertently may have hurt will forgive me, I wasn't myself! I'm free of my addiction now and I'm determined to stay that way for as long as I live.

Cheryl had told the media, after we had divorced, that I did not finish my rehab program and couldn't even do it for one month. This was not true, of course I finished it if I hadn't, I would never have gotten away from my addiction with prescription drugs! Not only did I finish that course, but I also kept in contact with the friends I met there for a long time afterwards. Her comments were not helpful to me or for our son as the news media has long memories and there are always old stories that will resurface. Did Cheryl even think about this before making her false statements?

My children are, for me, my anchor and I focused on them to be part of the means by which I would get away and stay away, from drugs. I did everything that was called on to me to do, by the people who were helping me back then. I left drugs and I became clean. I have been clean now, from my addiction with pain meds, for well over six years. In fact, I continued with the counselling program for a long time after I left the rehab facility, to make sure I remained away from drugs. If I hadn't stayed and completed the program, I would never have gotten free from my addiction with prescription drugs.

I also developed a strong friendship with my "teammates" at the rehab facility and I wasn't about to let them down as they too were looking to me to be strong for them as well as for myself. The only reason I left was because I was done with my addiction and it was time to pick up the pieces of my life and start again with my new life and my new me.

Cheryl and I are now living in different parts of the country, but we have remained friends and will always be friends regardless of our differences. Though I can't see my son as often as I would like, nevertheless, I had the chance to spend a whole summer in 2019 with our son, Antonio.

His full name is Antonio Kamakanaalohamaikalani a Hawaiian name. Our vacation together was very important to me and we both had a really great time together; time to bond and just hang out getting to know each other as father and son. That was for me what life is about, being able to spend time with my family! Remaining good friends after a divorce has meant I can still be a father figure to our son, which is important.

God works in mysterious ways.

Chapter 38

My Children

My three children have been and will always be everything to me and have been there for me no matter what. Our children are a gift from God.

Jack, my first son is my eldest, was born on August 6th, 1994. His mother Virginia Madson and I remained friends, following our divorce, so he could have a normal life. Virginia did a great job in bringing him up. Jack has a big heart and has boundless love for all people. Jack and I are very close and always will be. One big difference, Jack wanted to be a professional snowboarder and now lives in Alaska. He has a tattoo on his arm that says Jesus and he is a Christian as am I too. He went to the Los Angeles Film School and took a Bachelor of Science degree in Game Production and Design, but so far, has not chosen that as his career. He loves walking, hiking and is in a country he loves, Alaska where he can live his own dream, every day.

Mina Bree, was born on August 29th, 2002, to Kristine Rosetti and I   and is the apple of my eye! As I am writing my book Mina is now approaching her 18th birthday and is a "wild horse" She is tough and smart and will always do her own thing. I like to think her opinionated and loveable nature is what she will need to make it in whatever she chooses to do. She definitely has a strong line of Sabato blood in her and will, like my other two children Antonio and Jack, do whatever she chooses to do and I have no doubt whatsoever she will always succeed.

Antonio Kamakanalohamaikalani, (Hawaiian), was born on May 1st. 2011, is my youngest and was a gift from heaven that Cheryl and I never expected to have. As I am writing my book, Antonio is 9 years old and has a strong faith in Jesus, as we all have in my family. With Antonio it is apparent in everything he does. He is very spiritually awake and his faith guides him every day. Antonio often talks of his faith and is not shy in talking about it. I believe he was a gift from God for us. We don't know what he will decide to do, but being a Sabato, he will succeed in whatever he chooses.

Of the million words we speak to our children we hope just 10% will remain with them and teach them what they need to succeed.

Chapter 39

Ships Passing in The Night

Pamela Anderson

While I was at Malibu, in a surfing competition, we were all in the water, taking some waves and were in our wet suites when I first saw Pamela Anderson. I was single at that time and I was at a high point in my career, with no partner.

I had become a popular figure and I was very up front then and decided to just go straight up to her, like a lion, and ask her out for a date!

To my great surprise, she agreed! We met for dinner and had a great evening together. When I left the following morning, everything was cool, we were like two ships passing in the night.

Years later, after Virginia and I had separated, I went to a well-known restaurant on Robertson Boulevard, in Hollywood. The restaurant was on two floors, with a big dining room downstairs and a bar upstairs overlooking the dining room. It was a great place to be as there were many stars who were often there. I was at a table with some friends, when a friend of mine came over to our table and told me that Pamela was upstairs.

I excused myself from my table and went upstairs to see her. I walked over and we started talking as she was sitting at the bar. We clicked once again as we had before and in fact it was as if we had never parted so we started again right where we left off, several years before. Pamela looked stunning that night and I kept looking at her thinking how incredibly beautiful she looked and believe me she was perfection itself, looking like a goddess!

Anyway, my friends had taken me to the restaurant, so I had no car to get home in and there we were, chatting together, at the upstairs bar with no care for the time. I suddenly thought of a line that Marlon Brando had said to Marilyn Monroe, which was mentioned in a book I had read called *"The Songs My Mother Taught Me,"* about Marlon Brando's life. Marlon by the way, was always one of my favorite actors (after Tom Cruise).

After Marlon met Marilyn for the very first time, at the Academy Awards, he said," Listen, my place or your place!" That was all, no hello, or good evening or any other words, just that, "Listen, my place or your place." In the movie they went to his place and had an amazing night together.

That line came into my head right then and there, as if Marilyn was now sitting right in front of me, (Pamela was even more beautiful) so I thought I would try it too with Pamela. I did! I looked her straight in her eyes and said, "Look... my place or your place." We went to my place!

The following morning, we said our goodbyes and I didn't meet Pamela again for a long while. But once again, I kept our relationship very private, no photos, no paparazzi and no one knew about us. I tried to keep my private life very private and for the most part I succeeded.

Pamela is a very intelligent woman and was becoming more interested in all that was going on at the time in the news and in politics. We seemed to talk a lot about current issues that were important to her while we were together and I found her conversation very stimulating.

Not all relationships have to go somewhere and in many cases when we meet someone even for a very short time, we can have fun together and those times become memories we can keep and are just what they are, a chance meeting, like ships passing in the night. We can enjoy these chance meetings and remember them and I understand that. I can now share this with you and it's cool with me as I am sure it is for Pamela. We parted as good friends and we are friends still, even though we haven't met for a long time. Sometimes our circles just touch another's, for one brief moment, that's the mystery of life.

Ashely Judd

I had always been a big fan of Ashely Judd and loved her in *"Kiss the Girls,"* with Morgan Freeman and *"A Time to Kill,"* in 1998. In fact, I've seen all her movies and loved every one of them. She seemed to pick movies that suited her personality. Some were hard roles for her to play and I admired that about her. But she is an amazing actress and, in every movie I had seen her in, I can honestly say I loved her in all of them, what a true talent Ashely is.

I was in Toronto when we were shooting the *"The Big Hit"* in 1998 when the Toronto Film Festival was coming up. The organizers invited the entire cast to go to the film festival, to all the events and parties and all the things that were going on in Toronto. I have to say, Toronto is a fantastic city and there is so much to do there.

At that festival I met Brad Pitt at one of the events and told him about the movie we were shooting, which he thought was pretty cool.

I saw Ashely at one of the functions there also and as soon as I saw her, me being me, a brash, very up-front and probably over-confident me, I wanted to meet her. I went straight over to talk to her and we hit it off immediately. When I told her I loved her acting, she was genuinely surprised especially when I told her about specific scenes and roles that she had played. When any of us genuinely love someone's work it's easy to talk about it with them.

She is highly intelligent and passionate about her beliefs and told me she wanted to do more than just make films. One thing led to another we had dinner together that evening, we talked the whole time. She was fun to be with, it felt to me like I had known her for years. As much as we talked about all the movies she had been in, she also wanted to hear about the things I had done as well.

The following day we went our separate ways and that was cool with both of us. It was not meant to be anything more than what it was.

However, I saw Ashely once again, sometime later at the premier of a movie with Morgan Freeman, for the premier of her movie, *"High Crimes,"* we chatted once again but now we had both moved on.

I have to say that we got on very well and it felt to me like we were similar souls meeting once again. I learned that A brief friendship can be just that, nothing more nothing less, but still fun to experience.

Jennifer Love Hewitt

I first met Jennifer Love Hewitt, when she was quite young when she was a child actress and was working for the Disney Channel. We both happened to be at the same place during a movie junket. I met her again, in early 2000, when I took my son Jack to the dentist, of all things, in Beverly Hills. Virginia and Jack were living in Hollywood at that time and Virginia asked me to take him as she could not take him to the dentist that day. I was living in Marina Del Rey at the time so I picked Jack up and took him to the dentist only to see that Jennifer was there too.

I was wondering, looking at her perfect smile, why she was there, anyway, while I was waiting for Jack, Jennifer and I started talking and we eventually exchanged numbers. We dated for a while and it was fun, but we didn't have the intentions for anything long lasting. However, one evening, while we were dining in a restaurant, the paparazzi found us and clicked off a few shots that made the news.

After that unfortunate incident and after the photos appeared in the news, Jennifer told me she didn't want people to know about her relationship with me. I told her I didn't care what other people thought in the hope that she would agree with me, but she didn't. I called her several times after that, but she never returned my calls so we went our separate ways.

Our short relationship ended over a couple of Paparazzi photos before it ever really started! It was sometime later, when I saw her again at a promotional junket for "*The Bold and the Beautiful,*" a TV series I was in and she was there as well promoting her show "*The Ghost Whisperer.*"

I wanted to tell her everything was cool and I wanted nothing but the best for her, so I went up to her and told her just that and also that there were no hard feelings. She said she understood and felt the same way and she added it was never about me, but of course while it was nice that she said that we both knew it was exactly what it was about.

I loved Jennifer's smile and our time together, she was a great person to be with, albeit for only a short time. When we parted, we parted as friends. It was during these times that I found myself trying to find the right person to be with, to find someone to have a lasting relationship with. But as the line from a song says, I was looking for love in all the wrong places.

It was to be many years later before I finally found that person, my soul mate, the person I want to spend my life with. But more of that later. Sadly though, many people never do find that right person, so I am blessed to find my own someone special, my soul mate.

Finding the right person is worth waiting for, sometimes it can take a lifetime and sometimes never.

Chapter 40

The Indianapolis 500

When I was growing up, In Italy, my family had always been Formula 1 and Motor GP (Grand Prix) fans all our lives. As a boy I would go onto the racetracks and go around them whenever I could on my bike. Racing is in my family's blood and always will be.

I chose to be an actor, but if I hadn't chosen acting, I'm certain I would have been a Formula 1 race car driver. I love everything about racing, the crowds, the atmosphere, the smell of the cars on the track, the locations and most of all the race cars themselves. I loved knowing about their engines, how they performed, who was driving for which team and what each driver had achieved. You could say I am an avid fan of F1.

Whenever I had the chance, I would go on the racetracks and race Go-karts, nothing professional but just for the fun of it. When I was living in California, I went to every racetrack and whenever I could. I drove on them to get the "feel" of each track. Although I never really had much time to get into racing because my acting was keeping me extremely busy then.

Racing in the U.S. goes back as far as 1907, with the Vanderbilt Cup, but crowd control was a big problem back then when racing was at Long Island. In 1962 British Racing driver, Jim Clark raced in the U.S. and won in a Lotus. Graham Hill also raced in a BRM. These were the big names in Formula 1 back then and winning the F1 World Cup was a huge event.

In the early 70's, Formula 1 and Grand Prix racing in the U.S. was at a low point but in the late 70's James Hunt (UK) and Mario Andretti (Italy) raced in the U.S, along with Emerson Fittipaldi and many others. But since then, Formula 1 hadn't been in the U.S. for many years, until a re-emergence in 2000 occurred which was really a big deal to me.

In 2000 I found out that Formula 1 was coming to the famous Indianapolis Motor Speedway. Formula 1 racing took place in the U.S. at Long Beach, California and when I found out it was to be held at the famous Indianapolis 500 Speedway, I knew I had to be a part of this historical event as I had been to Indianapolis many times to watch the famous 500-mile race there. It was always held on Memorial Day Sunday.

My father and I went to Indianapolis and hung out with James Garner as they had both worked together in the award-winning movie *"Grand Prix,"* back in 1966 and had remained good friends ever since. We always had a great time at the Speedway also because the entire city, of Indianapolis, came alive for the Indianapolis 500.

For the entire month of May, Indianapolis and the homes around in the suburbs were decked out in black and white checkered flags, in all the shops, in people's front yards, on the street lampposts and from the city all the way down 16th Street to the motor Speedway, where the racetrack was. There were race day parties and big events all over Indianapolis. Signs all over the town and at Indianapolis International Airport said," Welcome Race Fans!" The crowds loved being there and so did we. People arrived at Indianapolis from all over the world for the biggest, most watched event in the world, The Indianapolis 500 Race.

It didn't matter what movie I was working on, the 500 was a trip I would never miss. We went to the Indy 500 Parade downtown, on the Saturday before the race, which was always held on the Monday of Memorial Day weekend. Indianapolis and the race crowd of some four hundred thousand people were all there with us to enjoy the event.

It was amazing to my dad and me and we loved Indianapolis which is still one of my favorite cities in the U.S. We were driven around the racetrack, in a convoy of cars, with other celebrities before the race. We waved at all the fans as our names were called out over the speaker system. We were driving around the track on Race-day before the race began and this was the highlight for me. We also hung out with racing icons and my father was friends with Phil Hill and Jacky Ickx, six times winner of the famous Le Mans Grand Prix.

While I was at the track, I was on the phone with Jackie Stewart who was also a good friend of mine and I knew my father would love to speak with him. I passed the phone over, so they could chat. It made me so happy to see my father chatting happily on the phone with Jackie Stewart, who was his hero. Jackie Stewart was someone my dad always said he would love to meet one day. Now at least Jackie Stewart and my father got to speak to each other, which was the next best thing!

My father, Antonio Sabato Sr. was in the famous movie "Grand Prix" starring James Gardner and Eve Marie Saint, which won three Academy Awards. So racing was, as I said, in our blood!

My father and I called in on the Mercedes team, their drivers were David Coulthard and Mika Häkkinen. That year, in 2000, Michael Schumacher was racing with Ferrari, so they were all coming to the Indianapolis speedway. I also came to Indianapolis that year and met with Tony George, who together with his family, owned the Indianapolis Motor Speedway.

I told them I wanted to race at the Speedway and told them I would do it for free. I would help promote the race, everywhere across the U.S. as Formula 1 was relatively unknown and people across the U.S needed to know more about Formula 1. They needed to know who the drivers were, how the racing went on and about the cars which were so much more advanced than the Indy Racing League (IRL) "open wheel" racecars.

This was a whole new style of track where the fans and drivers were used to oval track racing, but this was a much more intricate track design with bends and hairpins, as well as left and right-hand turns. Cars were made to brake and accelerate in rapid succession for the entire race and the cars were built to handle that type of racing. As for me? I made it known I just wanted them to help get in the race there!

I didn't hear anything for a long time until I was contacted by the McLaren Mercedes team to meet them at the track. My father and I are real Italians and we love Ferrari, so we turned up dressed all in Ferrari red! We were wearing red Ferrari racing jackets, red socks, red Ferrari shoes and there we were in the garage with the Mercedes team! But they were so gracious to us and they knew my dad from his movie *"Grand Prix,"* so we got a pass for wearing Ferrari colors!

I think this brought the best out of me and my dad, because with Formula 1 all we talked about was racing, the cars, the engines, the teams and the drivers. We were both truly knowledgeable about it. We not only talked about the racing but also about how to win points, the strengths of the teams we knew, even the more technical issues about the cars and the engines.

After the terrible events of 911, the race that year, in 2001, was moved to the end of September. This coupled with the problems swirling around the Michelin tires, when Ralf Schumacher (Michael's brother) crashed in practice driving on Michelin tires. It was determined that the tires they were using were not up to the constant stress of the fast driving and hard left and right-hand turns. This also badly impacted that first Formula 1 race at Indianapolis.

Sadly, these events and the disagreements about TV rights and TV coverage derailed the Formula 1 remaining at Indianapolis. I always thought that the F 1 track and the history with racing should have been a perfect match, but it is what it is, unfortunately.

In 2001, I started to promote the Grand Prix racing all across the Midwest, but when 911 happened it cast a big shadow across America. That year the race was postponed until September 30th. I had been at the racetrack in 2000 promoting the race and I became the spokesman and presenter at the F1.

Despite this and the fact that many were afraid to fly in a country still in shock, from 911, People still came, but that year the atmosphere was vastly different and understandably so. It was somewhat muted, not nearly as happy and excited as they had been in previous years. When the Airforce Jets did their flyover, as they always did at Indianapolis, spirits were lifted and people around me at the track that day thought, we can do this and we will get through this.

It was very emotional, for every single person at the track that year and I will always remember that race and the strength and determination of the people at Indianapolis racetrack and in the city of Indianapolis. The patriotism at the track was incredible and people were determined to pull together, as one, and I was there feeling very proud to be part of that patriotism.

I had my PR manager and a friend with me and I was on the radio stations making myself as visible as possible to get as much PR as I could for the race. I was also talking to all the teams there. There was the Porsche cup as well to promote so there was a lot going on.

We drove all over the Midwest, stopping at garages and radio stations to talk about Formula 1 being at Indianapolis. It was fun and I had on air debates with many people about the differences between Formula 1 and what they were used to with oval racetracks in the IRL League. I met so many great people especially Nascar fans, who are the biggest group of racing fans in the U.S. But when they heard about it from me, they began to understand it more and many became F1 fans as well. It was never a case of one or the other, but a case of both, being important for the American motor racing culture.

They began to understand when I told them about how the race is set up, the tires, the cars and how much a typical F1 racecar costs, which was in the millions of dollars. These cars are more like jet planes with wheels with all the technology inside them. But it was hard for me to promote Formula 1, as people here in the U.S. weren't used to Grand Prix racing and there were not enough fans in the U.S. to make it work financially to cover the cost of TV broadcasting.

All this along with the events that happened in September 2001, followed by the Michelin Tires debacle, when many drivers refused to use those tires, following problems they had with the tire compound. Sadly, it was the wrong time for Formula 1 to gain momentum at the Indianapolis raceway at that time. In the end, the Indianapolis Speedway was set up for the 500-mile race and I think it will be a long time before the F1 will be considered to be held there. Sometimes a series of unrelated events prevents what we want to happen, but that, as they say, is fate.

Racing at Indianapolis

To me, Michael Schumacher was to motor racing as Michael Jordan was to basketball and I knew him personally. I followed Formula 1 everywhere a race was held and I made sure I went to as many races as I possibly could. I mentioned that this was something I wanted to do, I wanted to race in the Porsche Cup and I wanted to do it at the world-famous Indianapolis Motor Speedway, where it was to premier there in Indianapolis.

I went to every single garage at the racetrack talking to the teams, the managers and the mechanics, asking them, "How do I get into this, how can I become a race car driver?" I asked them all if they needed another driver but I had no experience as a licensed racecar driver. I was determined to do this and I asked them," What do I need to do to be a racecar driver." I talked over and over again to the Porsche race team and must have got on their nerves because one day I got a call from one of their team. He told me I had to get a professional racing license before I could go on a racetrack or even be considered by them for a position on their team. They told me what I had to do and if I did these things, I should call them back and they would see me again.

I called Skip Barber, who had one of the best racing schools in the world, they have several schools on the East Coast, but I went to their school in Laguna Seca, in Salinas California, as it was closer to me.

Fortunately, they knew who I was and I told them I needed to get a professional license as soon as possible. I asked them what I needed to do to get started. They told me I had to take their three-day course and I also needed to race at different tracks to learn the skills required to be able to race without killing or injuring myself or others.

After a lot of driving on their track and learning what was required to become a race car driver, I eventually mastered the basics and implemented all they were teaching me. After many hours of practicing, I finally completed and passed their three-day course. After this I had to drive in three races, which I did as well, racing in three of the Skip Barber 3000 races.

I didn't do as well as I hoped I would in those races, but I was learning. I was determined to reach my goal of racing at Indianapolis so I raced in a few more challenges where I came in the top fifteen. Imagine that! I had just got my racing license and I was already racing, and I was well on my way to achieving my goal. But next, I had to get a Professional American Driver's License or SCCA License.

Sometime later, a manager from Porsche Racing called me and told me I should go to Stuttgart to race on their private test track to show my skills to their mechanics and technical staff there. Porsche Racing were in the big league, so of course I wanted to see how well I could manage on their test track. They would be looking at my speeds, timing, gear shifting, cornering, breaking, the lines I was taking driving around the track and my overall driving performance to see if I had what it takes.

The Stuttgart track is extremely difficult to do and that is probably why they wanted to see me drive there, which was a good thing. The track I was to drive on is where Porsche tests all their race cars, street cars and drivers.

I flew to Rome first as I had things to do there, then I flew on to Stuttgart. When I arrived, all my luggage was lost and I didn't get it until six months later when it arrived back in L.A. of all places. Anyway, they picked me up in Stuttgart as soon as I had arrived. They gave me their Nomex racing gear to wear while I drove their Porsche racecars around the track. It was exciting and such a pleasure to be there and I wondered how many famous drivers had been tested here and how many cars had driven around this test track.

I was excited and a little scared as well, not knowing what to expect when I met their technical advisor and their engineering staff who were there to help me and offer me advice.

I got in the car which was a professional GP3 race car with roll cage and all the technical parts found inside a Porsche race car. I was there with another professional driver, sharing the track, but he had more experience than me.

I have to say this was certainly one of the most difficult things I had ever undertaken and it took me hours and hours of driving, around the Porsche track, under the ever-watchful eye of the Porsche technical group there at the track, working with me, correcting my many, many, mistakes, before I was even close to understanding what was required to become a racecar driver.

I made a lot of mistakes and had to keep re-starting after listening to their advice on what I was doing wrong each time I went back to the pits. I got the chance to watch another driver who was learning the same as me. He went out on the track first and I could tell by the way he drove he knew what he was doing. I could see this from the telemetry that they were using to check on all his gear changes, acceleration blips, breaking and fast acceleration along the straightway.

Then it was my turn, to test and put into practice all I had learned. I got in and despite all I had been shown, I pushed the car too hard on one of the bends and ended up sliding off the track and on to the grass. There was no damage to the car, but after I brought it back in I remember seeing the look on the technical advisor's face. He looked very sternly at me and pointed his finger saying, "If you do that again! If you do that again! you are never going to Indianapolis!" He then told me, "I want you to get back in the car and I want you to do exactly what I tell you and I want you to show me what you've got." I said, "Yessir I'll do just that!" feeling very humble and a little stupid.

I got back in the car, regained my composure, took some deep breaths, thought again about what they had taught me and started to drive the track but now listening intently to what he was telling me. I knew the track a little better as I had been around it several times now, but this time I had learned a big lesson. I followed all I had been told and I was more careful, which sounds strange, as I was going as fast as I could, but now with better control.

Make no mistake, this was no breeze; this was me putting a lot of things together simultaneously while driving at speeds of over 180 miles per hour. I was learning how to take the bends, both left and right-handers, where to accelerate, where when and how to brake; how and when to change gears up and down and how to get the "line" right each and every time. This is not for everyone; it can be a life-or-death situation. Just one small mistake at these high speeds can be fatal.

But, when I finished, I had learned a lot and I finally earned my SCCA license from the Porsche racing team! After that in 2002 and 2003, my dream was finally coming true, I was racing on the Indianapolis 500 Speedway! I was driving my dream at the world-famous Indianapolis Motor Speedway, as a professional driver with a professional team and, only three years after I made my decision to do it!

I want to tell you all who read my book that believe me a dream can be achieved by anyone who has a dream to do something you have never done before, but are determined to do, something that is very different or special or even a place you want to go to. If you work at your dream and imagine your dream coming true, as I did here, you can make it happen. All it takes is for you to, "Make It Happen!" as I did here.

The Indianapolis Motor Speedway

I finally made it to the starting grid, on that famous Indianapolis Motor Speedway, looking back in my mirror at all the cars around me waiting for the start of the Porche race and the hundreds of thousands of people in those famous Indianapolis Raceway stands all there watching. I was nervous and excited at the same time and my adrenalin was kicking in sharpening my senses.

In my first race I was what they call a "rookie" I finished in the top twenty, out of twenty-six cars, which was not bad considering I had never raced there and with such a full field. In my second race there, they gave me a brand new "GT3 Cup Car" to race, I didn't do as well then but for me it was more about being there. During the race it was raining and conditions were very difficult to drive in.

It had been pouring with rain earlier and the spray coming up from the cars, around and in front of me, made it difficult to see anything at all, especially at over 160 mph. The feel of the car, the lines I had to take on the bends, the braking and the "Ceiling" of the car were all very different because of this and I had not had the chance to learn how to drive on a wet track in the pouring rain.

Now, though I know I am a much better racecar driver in the rain, snow, or dry tracks because I now have more experience. I have kept on racing, I have raced open wheel, stock cars, Go Karts, and even four-wheel drives. If I knew then what I know now I would have done a lot better. But isn't that racing and isn't that life?

I also did celebrity races in Melbourne, Australia and if anyone asked me now to race, I would say yes, even if I've never raced that track or in a car I hadn't tried yet. I would always say "yes I'd love to!" I've now raced the IndyCar, Global Tuner Grand Prix and GT3 Super Cup.

I've tested and raced many different race cars in my life, from salon cars to open wheel cars and the GT3 cars.

I now know nearly all the major racetracks in the world. I could even draw most of them and I know their strengths and difficulties because I follow motor sports all the time, it's my passion and always has been.

I did what I wanted to and succeeded, despite never having done this before and I had so much fun along the way, doing what I wanted to do and "stretching" my limits while accepting the challenge in doing it! I will continue to race cars for as long as I possibly can, it's in my blood and I love it!

I can honestly say that for me, this is what life is all about, doing something that stretches my abilities to see what I can achieve. I never dreamed I would be able to drive at the Indianapolis Motor Speedway in a real race, it took me three years to achieve my dream and it was the greatest experience of my life!

As an interesting anecdote, I was in an episode of CSI NY, when I crashed and burned in an explosive episode. It was reported as "he is passionate about racing and is joined by Danica Patrick, the first woman to win an IndyCar race" for that episode.

In the show, I played racing legend Davi Santos, who two days before a Grand Prix Race dies in a car explosion on the streets of Manhattan. When the "CSI: NY" team investigate, they discover that the car was tampered with and Danica's character, Liza Gray, who is Davi's main competitor, becomes the prime suspect.

I learned that with determination I could achieve almost anything I set my mind to do.

Chapter 41

A Tribute to my friend Herb Ritts Jr.

(Herb Ritts August 13, 1952 – December 26, 2002)

Meeting the legendary Herb Ritts did so much to help further my career back in the early days when I first began my career. He and I became close personal friends, after he had taken so many of the most famous photos of me for Calvin Klein along with the video he shot for Janet Jackson's *Love Will Never Do (Without You).* I had been many times to his beautiful home in Malibu. Herb had taken some of the best and most stunning photographs in the world. His technique of light and composition was his art and was unsurpassed by any other photographer.

I saw Herb again later at a gala event for The American Foundation for Aids Research (amfAR) which was the nation's leading non-profit organization dedicated to the support of AIDS research. This was a foundation that Herb played a big part in supporting. He went to conferences and was very vocal and public in his support of Aids research. He took so many beautiful photos of people he knew who were suffering with Aids and his photographs left an indelible imprint for all who saw them.

With his beautiful and caring photographs, he succeeded in bringing Aids to the forefront of millions of people's minds and he helped overcome the stigma associated with this devastating disease. Not so much for the deadly disease, that it was, but for showing the pain and suffering of those who had contracted it.

I remember reading about the famous tennis player Arthur Ashe, who while at the top of his tennis career and after making a world-wide name for himself as one of the world's greatest tennis players, he contracted Aids from a contaminated blood transfusion of all things. Arthur Ashe brought this to the forefront because up to then people had limited awareness of aids.

No one knew that Herb was suffering from Aids himself and I certainly never saw anything to indicate he was sick when we were together.

He was a very private person and kept himself to himself. He was also quirky and I loved that about him. He would wear the same style T shirt and jeans every day and his closet comprised of dozens of pairs of Levi 501's, all he wore were black and the same Calvin Klein black T shirts. That was all he wore, black and black. It didn't matter where he was and every time, I saw him he was always wearing black. It was through Herb Ritts that I met Madonna.

When the news came out that Herb had passed away, it came right out of the blue and I was shocked and saddened at the news. Herb sadly passed away on December 26th, 2002, at the age of only fifty years old. I remember thinking, at least my friend got to see his last Christmas day. The news quickly flashed around the world spreading to all the countries his worldwide fame had taken him to, as well as the famous names he had worked with in his life-long career as one of the world's top photographers.

The great things he had done, not only as a photographer but also his videos, were now of even more interest to the entire world and all those who had been touched by his art. He photographed campaigns for Giorgio Armani, Chanel, Donna Karan, Calvin Klein, and Gianni Versace among many others.

Following his death, his incredible photographs were shown in memorial exhibitions worldwide and were amongst the best and most visited exhibitions ever. Herb Ritts left us with his own foundation, *"The Herb Ritts Jr. Foundation"* in California.

I look at the many photos that he took of me, even now, so many years on, and I still feel so privileged that my friend, Herb Ritts, took them. I am honored to have been able to call Herb Ritts, my friend and I have many of the original photos he took of me, I keep them as a memory, my personal tribute of the time I spent with my beautiful friend, Herb Ritts.

Working with Herb Ritts was an honor and I will never forget my beautiful and quirky, friend!

Rest In Peace, my friend, Herb Ritts

Chapter 42

Reality Shows

I was invited to some reality TV shows that were a lot of fun to be part of. One of these reality shows was called *"My Antonio"* which VH1 wanted to do with me in 2009.

The series followed me in my search for a partner, not in real life of course, but it was just for the show. Single women were invited to meet me in Hawaii, to compete for my approval, imagine that! Extra drama in the show was created by the addition of my mother and the appearance of my ex-wife, Tully Jenson, as one of the contenders. In the first show I swam ashore and immediately dismissed one of the women because I didn't like her hands and feet (of course not in reality I have to add). The remaining ladies had to climb up Mount Pu' U' in a show of determination for me.

They allowed me to put the girls, who were with me in the show who were contending to be my new partner, through various tests, doing whatever I wanted them to do just having fun for the show. Critics called the show *"The Bachelor on steroids!"*

As for the show being reality, it wasn't! Every scene was staged and planned ahead of time, with me and with the contenders. There was no "Reality" in the show at all, it was for pure entertainment. But it was so much fun to do, as they had my mom on the show, looking like Sophia Loren, with big hats and looking very glamorous and she loved it!

My Mom wasn't even Italian, she was originally from Prague (this is another story), but it didn't matter to them, as long as she played the part. My mom was told exactly what to say and the show worked. When they brought my ex-wife Tully Jensen, to stir up the pot, it did just that in the show and we were all having such a lot of fun coming up with ideas, conjuring up plots and schemes to make the show more entertaining.

In the show Tully moved into the suite with the rest of the women and was greeted with suspicion. There was a feeling, from one of the contenders, that Tully was really my sister! Then I organized a "My Antonio" workout to test the ladies' physical mettle. I also had to test their romantic spirit by having them write love-letters to me.

Money was no problem for the show's producers, they gave me a helicopter and a motorbike to use when we were filming and we filmed all over beautiful Hawaii. My Mom had a great time with me and with the people on the show. I was having a great time too with the girls that came to compete to be my new partner. But each day when filming was finished, we went back to our rooms and hung out with our kids which made the whole experience more personal for the family man that I am.

I spent time fitness training for myself, as well as training the director and the crew getting all of them fit and they loved it. Eventually we had the fittest crew in the business! Some of the crew were overweight when we started filming, they lost weight while working with me on that set. My early morning routines were really working well for them, even if they had been out late the night before.

The girls on the show were, for me, just for the show and I had no interest in any of them other than the parts they played with me for the show. I got to vet each contestant beforehand, so I knew who they were before they arrived on-set. It was a "made for TV" reality show and as I said, nothing was real at all. But nevertheless, we all had a great time and it was fun doing it. I really enjoyed all the things I got to do with them and as an added bonus, I had my family with me while we were shooting the show, so it was like being paid to be on a paid family vacation!

I have no doubt that many who watched the show thought the activities were real and probably they were hoping I would choose one of the girls to be my partner (their own favorite). But as I have said the show was just that, a non-reality- reality show and we all enjoyed being in it and making it look like reality. There is no such thing as a reality show, they are not reality at all, but what they are is pure entertainment and I loved playing my part purely as entertainment.

Building Boots and Dancing Shoes!

There are degrees of difficulty in everything we do, but some of the difficulties, in movies and TV shows, are more fun than others! In 2014, I was doing another reality show called *"Fix It and Finish It."* This was a reality series about re-modeling people's homes. In this case we really were doing what was shown as "Reality TV". We were in a different city for every show and we were helping people, couples and families, who needed help fixing up or remodeling their homes, RVs, and cabins. We were actually doing the building renovation work on the show. We ripped out walls, fixed roofs, bathrooms, kitchens, gardens and anything they had written into the show that needed to be rebuilt, fixed up, or re-modeled.

I really enjoyed the work, especially the before and after, when the owners who had written in, to the show and were lucky enough to be chosen, were so genuinely delighted with the results of what we had completed for them and all the viewers could see this at the end of each show. The show involved me helping my team of builders while walking each job through from start to finish.

Dancing With the Stars

At the same time, I was doing that show, some of my close friends had been watching *"Dancing with the Stars,"* and thought I should get on the show. At first, I said "no way!" But after a while when I had watched several of those shows, I thought of the challenge in doing something completely new, so I asked my agent to call them at ABC. He did and they asked me to come on the show and just like that I was on the show!

I was going to dance with none other than Emmy nominated Cheryl Burke. Cheryl was a professional dancer who had her own dance studios. I have to say here she was a hard task master. Our personalities did not always get along, but nevertheless, I did appreciate her teaching me to dance and gradually I learned different dance steps that I had never danced before; the Foxtrot, the Rumba, the Salsa, the Waltz and I was becoming reasonably proficient with each of these dances.

Cheryl had won *"Dancing with the Stars"* twice, dancing with Drew Lachey, of 98 Degrees and with Emmitt Smith the retired football player. She had even taught Drew Carey, the game show host, to dance up to a professional level. So, I thought if they can do it, I can give it my best shot too.

The hard part was that I was also still doing the show, *"Fix It and Finish It."* So, in order to do both shows, I had to fly straight from the building site, wherever we were filming, to the dance studio to train with Cheryl, swapping my builders boots for my dancing shoes.

I had a team of builders working with me at the same time and they became friends and relied on me to help make the show a success. In the mornings, I was the builder, ripping up floors, walls, ceilings, humping building materials in and out of houses and later, the same day, I was the dancer in dancing shoes and smart clothes!

One minute I was in in jeans and working boots and the next I was in dancing pants and patent leather dancing shoes! I was their only celebrity, back then, to have two shows running at the same time and I can promise you it was hard work.

I was doing *Fix It and Finish It*, in New Orleans and we were finishing all the shows that week. Cheryl flew out to meet me, so I was working on *Fix It and Finish It* in the mornings, then I went to meet Cheryl in a dance studio to dance, then I would go back to *Fix It and Finish It* later that same day!

On Thursdays, I would fly from New Orleans to LA, to rehearse, Friday, Saturday and Sunday, each weekend then record the show which was then filmed "live" on Mondays. Then, Monday night when the show finished filming, I flew back to the location for *Fix It and Finish It*. I did this for two months solid. I loved the challenge but at the end I was ready to take some time off!

Cheryl told me several times, "when you are Dancing, Antonio, you have to put everything else out of your mind if you are to become a great dancer." She pushed me to the limit and it didn't matter to her what else I was doing, at the same time. I know she was very frustrated with me, but we worked at it together and together, we made it a success.

I'm Italian, which means I am often impulsive, sometimes boisterous with strong opinions and passionate about what I am doing. Several times I was ready to walk away, as we were both hard-headed. But then Cheryl was a professional and she was doing the right thing by pushing me hard to succeed. There was no softening up in her methods. I also knew she was relying on me, not to make her look bad, so walking away was really not an option. I didn't like the anger and the hard push, which was Cheryl's method, that was why I never went into the military. But her method worked!

The dances were hard for me to learn to a competitive standard. Another coincidence was that I was married to a Cheryl who was a Filipino and I was dancing with another Cheryl who was also a Filipino! One was more than enough but two and both were determined women!

The great thing about those shows was that my mom, my stepdad and my children were there to watch me dance. On the day of the competition, Cheryl took me to one side and said, "Look Antonio, whatever happened this week, put it out of your mind and have fun, whatever you do, have fun." What she told me worked and what you see is me smiling and doing my best, which was for real.

As we progressed upwards, in the contest, we had to do two dances in each show and we also had to change partners, making it even more difficult! We had a little time to learn with our new partner and we were training in Memphis. I was still doing my other show *Fix It and Finish It*, so I went to the practice studio, took off my work boots and put on my dancing shoes to switch roles from builder to dancer. Talk about two opposite sides of the work spectrum and here I was doing it.

On the day of the filming for the show, we both had fun and our smiles were real! We got through seven rounds, which I thought was a great achievement and better than I thought we would do.

We eventually lost to **Alfonso Ribeiro**, who was a great guy and a superb dancer. Alfonso had learned tap dance when he was a young boy and he had even danced with Michael Jackson. Although I never liked losing, I had to admit he was the real deal and he deserved to win.

After two months of doing both shows, I became sick as I had been pushing myself too hard doing two shows simultaneously.

I really appreciated all Cheryl did to "bring up my game" and all her efforts with me showed results I never thought I could achieve and certainly it was a lot better than I expected. *Dancing with The Stars* is a great entertainment machine with over fourteen years as a popular and highly visible show, I was fortunate to have been given the chance to compete.

Cheryl and I came 8th with a score of 28.6, which I thought was pretty good...for a builder! I learned that we could look back at things we have done and just smile at the ridiculousness of those things we did in our past!

Stars In Danger

Another reality show Fox wanted me to take part in was a program they were running called *"Stars in Danger,"* about placing well known stars in difficult situations where they would face danger. These were real life situations and were no joke to do. There was of course training from the various experts in whatever field of expertise was required for the show and each dangerous situation would be the basis for the next episode. The episode they wanted me to be in was diving from an Olympic diving board!

The diving board was 15 meters, or around 50 feet high and I took lessons from an expert trainer. But when they started training at

UCLA, several of the stars and celebrities, who had also agreed to take part, got hurt. Two left and, not surprisingly, never came back. One was the actor and game show host, Joey Lawrence (Win Lose Or Draw), the other was Joey Conseco, the famous baseball star, who was the first ever to hit 40 home runs and steal 40 bases in one season.

Who do they call when they don't have enough celebrities for a show? They called me of course, to fill in the spot which had now become vacant, probably because so many stars had declined to dive after seeing how dangerous it was. I asked them when the competition was going to be shown on TV, they told me it was less than two weeks! "Two Weeks!" They called me on a Tuesday and the show was to be filmed the following Friday, it was just over one week away, in fact, I had only eleven days to get this!

However, me being me said, OK I'll do it, just like that! As you have no doubt already guessed, I'll try anything once and I love a challenge. So, I went to the Olympic Pool every day and I was taught not just how to dive, but how to dive like an Olympic diver! And in only ten days! Yeah right I would be at that standard when the Olympic divers have practiced since childhood. But one thing for certain, I would give it my best as I always do!

We were to be filmed at the Chelsey Piers Olympic pool, in Connecticut, in front of a crowd of people including their TV cameras for the program. I was to learn two main dives; one was diving with a partner in a double synchronized dive and the second dive was solo. My diving partner was Terrell Owens the well- known football player and the former NFL Wide Receiver, who played for 16 seasons. He held or shared several NFL records and ranked third in career receiving yards.

We were doing the double dive together, but I wanted to win the singles diving contest as this was me and me alone and succeed or fail, at least I could do this by myself.

After all the training, all ten days of it, which was mainly us getting used to the height of the diving board, we were as ready for the dive or a ready as we would ever be. Terrell and I, braced ourselves, successfully completed the synchronized dive and we were both more than a little nervous. Then it came to my solo dive. I closed my eyes, while standing on the very high diving board, and prayed quietly that I would do ok and not screw it up. My adrenaline was now on full alert!

My dive went very well and I actually won the singles diving event for real. It was very cool to win that event and I was both happy and surprised that I did the dive solo and won the event.

However, at the end of the program I had so many bruises all over my body I looked a mess. I had the most bruises I had ever received, even more than when I was doing my own stunts in the low budget films when they couldn't afford a stuntman!

This was part of my personal drive for success, I would try anything at all, to see how much I could achieve and I was fearless to try things like this.

I would never do this again, but I did it once and that was enough!

Chapter 43

Hard Roles to Play

When an audience watches a movie they are only interested in what they see and hear on the silver screen, which is as it should be. Though these days it's more often on their TV's or Tablets, rather than physically going to see these movies on the big screen, which is perfectly OK and it keeps the mystery of the art available to a wider audience.

When I have agreed to play a role, I act exactly as the Director wants and if I have questions about a specific role, I go through it before the shoot begins. A difficult role becomes a real challenge for any of us but, we rise to that challenge and do what is asked of us. In the movie, *"Drifter,"* I was the serial killer, *Henry Lee Lucas* and I played the lead role as Henry himself. The movie was based on a real-life person.

My part was very dark and it disturbed me to play him. I felt bad playing him as I knew each murder, my part in the movie played, was based on a real person who had been murdered. I was re-enacting each murder based on news and police reports of each crime. This was going through my mind with every scene. I did not feel good at the end of each day's filming and had to keep telling myself it was just a movie, but at the same time I knew each murder had been a real event.

I played many different roles, in comedies, murder movies, as street fighters, EMT's, in sci fi movies and with each role I played, there was always the hope I would land that one key role, where I would be seen as both a serious and capable actor. I was able to be flexible enough to play many roles and in fact, writing this book forced me to remember details of my many movies and TV shows I had been in. Some of the work I did never made it to the screen and other work I have done has never been seen, but that is the movie business.

Some Movies Don't Hit the Mark

In many of the movies I was in, I was convinced the movie would make it and some I thought would make it big. But not one movie I was in, ever did make it big. Was I being cast more for my looks? Even *Earth 2*, which was expensive to produce and had the backing of Steven Spielberg behind it, but despite this, it didn't last more than one season. This was a lesson for me to learn and as I have said earlier, I've made mistakes along the way, but each time I picked myself up, I overcame that difficulty and I moved on as we all must!

We are not all wired the same way and some sadly use their defeats as a reason for not trying or moving on to succeed. That is not me and never will be, I will always keep trying. I knew that making movies was expensive and costs are calculated by the hour. There is a camera crew, lighting, assistants, scripts, other actors and many people are involved, from start to finish, so any movie is a team effort from start to finish.

Even after a movie has been completed, there is the selling of that movie to distributors and TV Networks and there is no guarantee it will even make it to the screen. I couldn't even guess now just how many films, after completion, have never been seen. It's a high-risk high reward business.

To get this into perspective, according to a WGA (Writers Guild of America) movie database roughly 50,000 screenplays are registered at the WGA each year but double this number are written. Many are dropped before ever being submitted.

So, out of as many as 100,000 professionally written screenplays, with a final 4,000 possibly good scripts written by as-yet-unknown writers, so the odds are only 4 out of all these 50,000 screenplays will actually sell and become movies. So, the chances are very slim indeed that a movie will even make it to the screen and even less that will make it to be successful. Then there is an even slimmer chance that it will then make it in the box office. As an actor, we take the risk when we agree to be in a movie, the risk it may bomb and take us all down with it.

It's always the public who decide the success of a film or TV series and that is as it should be!

Chapter 44

The Other Side of Movies

It was 2014 and I was in a Christmas movie with Shannen Doherty, *All I Want for Christmas.* It was a great movie, but none of the crew, actors, assistants and in fact none of us were paid for our work.

One day as we were filming a scene, a stranger came barging onto the set, right in the middle of the shoot and started shouting saying, "I want my money, gimme my money I want it right now!" We had to stop filming, we didn't know what to do and I had never seen anything like this on a movie set, but hell, shit happens!

We were all on fairly standard film contracts and mine was a weekly contracted sum, but we couldn't get hold of the producer to pay us. Someone on the set called SAG (Screen Actors Guild) and we had to sign a lot of papers and fill out forms, so they would go after him to get our money. I was angry, not only for myself, but especially for the young actor who was playing my son. His name was Mason Douglas and he was playing *Jason Patterson* in that movie.

He was an amazing young actor and it seemed so bad not to pay him. I thought at the time how bad Mason must have felt, working so hard to be good in this movie and then not to get paid. I knew Mason's family as they lived near me at Thousand Oaks. I enjoyed making the film and it was great working once again with Shannen, she told me about all the things she had done in the two years since we had last worked together.

I always loved working with kids in movies they were to me almost like extended family, that I got to know when they were present on the set, as the filming went on. I helped them with their lines, played games, goofed around and answered their many questions about movies when there was nothing to do.

Around a year and a half later, SAG caught up with the director of that movie and called me, to let me know they had found the missing director, but all they got for me was $500 which didn't even cover my airfare to get to that set! So much for SAG and their ability to help. Still, it was better than a poke in the eye with a blunt stick!

But, as I've said before, "That's showbiz!" Sometimes we have to be prepared for the unexpected.

A contract must be honored by both parties otherwise it is just words.

Chapter 45

My Friend, Cameron Boyce

One very sad story I want to include, more as a tribute to a wonderful young actor and friend I had the pleasure to work with. His name was Cameron Boyce. He played the part of my son, in *"General Hospital Night Shift."* The show lasted for two seasons and was filmed for night-time audiences.

Cameron was an amazing young actor with great talent and was destined to go far and to do great work. The part Cameron played was a recurring role, as my son, his name in that movie was "Stone" after my brother in the film. Cameron frequently had seizures in the movie and in one scene I had to tell him to go to bed, but he falls to the floor with a seizure and nearly dies in my arms.

Recently in 2019 I saw that this lovely boy who had worked so hard in everything he had done, who had a great career ahead of him and who I loved working with, had passed away following a very bad seizure. Cameron made his acting debut in the horror film *"Mirrors"* at just 9 years old. Two years later, he appeared in the blockbuster Adam Sandler flick, *"Grown Ups,"* as one of Sandler's children.

It made me so sad and I spent a lot of time thinking about him and his lovely family who I had got to know on that film set several years earlier. Rest in Peace, my very young, young friend, I loved working with you my friend Cameron Boyce. You will always have a special place in my heart.

Some people we meet become treasured memories long after they are gone.

Chapter 46

Doing What We Must

When my career was at a low ebb, I chose to do some movies that, upon looking back, were not great movies. But, when you have no money coming in, you must do whatever it takes to earn enough money to put food on the table.

Some of the movies I acted in or agreed to do, I don't want to name them, were less than perfect for me but that also is the business. "'I'm acting!" We can argue that all movies are in fact works of art and the beauty of art is after all in the eye of the beholder.

Anyway, I did whatever I had to do to make ends meet. I did parts in movies that were not good movies, as far as the critics reported, but at the time it was all I could get and as I said earlier, we never know how a movie will be accepted or if it is a well-made movie. Critics look at the name of the movie, the way it's put together, its success or failure in the box office and sometimes they make us all believe that actors, like me are complete failures, if we are seen in a less than perfect movie. It's like an immediate and constant switch, one day the switch is on and we are doing great, the next day, the switch is off and we are a complete failure, but that again, is the movie business.

We all have to do what is necessary to make enough money to live and to pay the bills and often this can lead to accepting roles in movies that may not end up being as popular as they were planned to be. When we are in movies like these, that, after their release, don't cover the high cost of production, as actors we are often the ones to blame.

This was the case with *"Earth 2,"* produced by Steven Spielberg. You would think that with his name it would be a smash hit and as I said earlier the trailer alone cost ten million dollars to make. Yet, after that first season it never continued to a second season. At the end of the day it is you my reader, you the audience, who ultimately decides what will fail and what will succeed. I have to add here that critics also play a big part in a movie's success or failure with the reviews they state on shows and in print.

But regardless, the audience always has the last say in the success or failure of any work of art, be it movies, books or artworks.

Tough decisions can have tough consequences!

Chapter 47

"One Nation Under God"

In 2017 I was going through another very tough time in my life. My divorce with Cheryl was being finalized, I was paying for a house I wasn't living in, but Cheryl was there with our son Antonio III, which was fine with me as I was living with my mother while I was getting through this difficult time after all the film work had dried up.

I needed work and I even put myself on Linked In, stating that I was looking for acting work. Can you imagine doing this, after all I had done with more than 90 movies and TV shows, but I had to do what I had to do.

One of the many calls I made was to the Casting Director Joey Paul Jensen, who responded to me through Linked In. She told me she had nothing at that time. But then a few days later she called me back and told me they were casting for a movie and could include me in the auditions if I was interested and, if I was, I could meet the producers and the director.

The movie was called, *"One Nation Under God,"* and I told her I was interested. However, as I read the script, I realized it was reflecting exactly me and my beliefs. What was happening was like a miracle and I knew, as soon as I read it, I just had to land the role.

The script was about unity, in the United States and about the "Pledge of Allegiance." In many parts of the script, almost word for word, it said the same words as my speech at the Republican National

Congress in Cleveland. That speech was from my heart and I was saying the same words to that huge audience, *"We should be united as a nation,"* and this role I hoped to play, as Senator Viera, was perfect for me.

I went for the audition and gave it all I had as I always did. This time though there was something else, something I couldn't explain, something that I felt was driving me forward to be in this movie. I said to the producers and the director, Lisa Arnold, "look I know you're looking for someone more famous than me to play this part, but I can play this with my eyes closed, this part is me!" I was blunt but I knew I was right!

As things worked out, they told me there was another actor they were looking at for the role and if I wanted to, I could do another part where some celebrities have a walk on scene.

The other actor was Neil McDonough and he was well suited to play this part too. I told them no, despite the fact I was desperate for work, I wouldn't to do that, I was not doing a walk on part. I didn't care to do that and although Neil was a friend and we had worked together before, he had other commitments and specific demands for doing the part, but they didn't want to wait until Neil could be free to commence.

Sometime after that meeting, when I thought I may not get the part, I continued to work out every day, as I always did, trying to keep busy, looking for work every day from first thing in the morning until well into the evening.

But later, after the final audition, I got a call from Joey and I was treading on eggshells, holding my breath, hoping it might be good news. She told me that Neil was unable to do this movie as he had other commitments and couldn't make it work. They then told me if I wanted it, the role of Senator Viera, was mine!

Finally! The part I wanted, in the movie I wanted to be in with a passion, was mine! I had to ask her again if I had landed the role because there were so many things going around in my head. Joey confirmed it saying she would call me when production started.

I can tell you that, landing this role was for me a miracle. It was not only because I desperately needed work and the money, but it was in a film that was about the same beliefs I had, beliefs borne out of my own life and my family's experiences, in their life. Those same beliefs were what I had stood up for at that rally in 2016 and told the world about, my message was about "unity."

"One Nation Under God" is the story about the political situation, right here, right now in America. The story is about a student who boldly stands up for God when a Presidential candidate visits his school. The exchange goes viral challenging both to step out in faith and to be the men that God has called them to be. It's also about bringing God back into our daily lives and creating a more unified America as it used to be, one flag, one nation living in harmony once again, under God with the freedom to say our pledge of allegiance in public places.

The film is also about the forces trying to pull our nation apart and the people who are doing it by sewing hatred for anyone who has an opinion that disagrees with theirs. The twisting of the truth to prove their point and their singular and intolerant point of view that is happening right now and it is tearing America apart.

My own political platform was about unity and a unified America with two opposing views but living in tolerance and harmony. Is there anything wrong with that? Surely people who have a view different to mine can accept my right to freedom of speech, the same as theirs, without trying to destroy my career as has now happened to me.

This movie was really a mirror reflecting on my own life, as it has become and reflected all I also believed in. It was so close to who I am, that as I was first reading the script and then, when I was acting the part of Senator Viera, it was as if I was living the part for all I truly believed in.

Nowadays, it is not cool to publicly say God this, or God that, when we are talking to others or to bring the word Jesus into a discussion. Isn't it strange that the name God appears in so many places especially on public, government, or legal buildings, yet the word Jesus appears almost nowhere? Yet it was he who died for us?

Reading that script was like a sudden realization that this was at the core of what I was now seeing happening to me. I was reading a script about someone telling a story, but it was my story too. The film was about the battle between freedom of speech and a schoolboy's wish to pray or say the Pledge of Allegiance if he wanted to. My part, as Senator Viera, had to make the difficult decision to help to win his freedom to say the "Pledge of Allegiance" if he chose to do so.

I prayed every day for God to let me have this one role in this one film and I prayed as hard as I had when I wanted to get off drugs when I knew I could never get free by myself without seeking a higher power.

I knew this movie was perfect for the time, here in America with the polarization between our two political parties and their respective followers. In particular with the platform, I stood on for my speech at the RNC for Republican nomination was the same as this roll I was to play in *One Nation Under God*.

I cried with relief on hearing the good news that I had the part and it was such a perfect role that may only come once in our lifetime. I gave my mom who was next to me a huge hug and I thanked God for helping me to get this part, in this movie and at this time in my life when I needed it the most. Divine intervention or just coincidence? I was now able to pay child support, pay my bills and insurance for my family and all began to get back on track for me, it was like a miracle!

As I see it, this is how God works, not in a blinding flash of light but in the way He put things in place giving us choices along the way, while building up to the end point when it all becomes so clear at the right time. When, after everything, we have made the right choices. As it says in the bible, *"All will become clear."* Again, coincidence or "Divine Intervention?" You can believe it was pure coincidence but really? Placing an ad in LinkedIn then getting the response for a role in a movie which was exactly what I ran for congress on was, to me, more than a pure coincidence.

I gave *"One Nation Under God"* the best performance I have ever given in any performance I have undertaken before, as a thankfulness for getting this part.

As I am writing this, I am very happy with the part I played under the superb direction of Lisa Arnold. Under her direction, each scene was perfect and I can honestly say I played my role, of *Senator Viera,* from my heart and soul as I believe what is happening right here, in the country I love, is destroying everything I believed was America. "Land of the free," and the film was dealing with exactly this.

The movie has received 32 awards at film festivals over the past year, underscoring the film's excellence and relevance to events happening right now. These awards, *One Nation Under God* had won, were all before the film was even released to the public.

For many reasons I hope this film becomes a huge success and I hope it wins more of the critical acclaim, it deserves, because it would validate the fact that there are still millions who love the message of "unity in America," under the Pledge of Allegiance, which still holds true today. *One Nation Under God* was released in 2020.

This was one part I had to play as it represented all I believe in, freedom of speech and standing for what any of us believe in.

Chapter

Photos
with My
Celebrity Friends

Many of these photos were taken by my mother Yvonne.

Me on *Fox and Friends Breakfast* with Steve Doocy, Ainsley Earnhardt, Brian Kilmeade, and Geraldo Rivera.

Having fun with the hosts of the Fox breakfast show.

I was on *The View* talking about my modeling work for
Calvin Klein.

Unveiling the 90ft poster of me on Time Square, for Calvin Klein.
I'm standing up high in front of the poster.

With my favorite actor and language consultant, Tom Cruise

With Valentino, fashion designer.

With my mom Yvonne on the Red Carpet at the
Oscars.

With Judge Jeanine.

With Maria Schriver.

My Mom and I with Martina Navratilova and my kids Jack and Mina.

With Jay Leno, we shared a love for cars and racing.

Above with Albert II, Prince of Monaco.

With Michael Jordan.

With Liza Minnelli.

With Madonna.

At the Oscars, with Daniel Day Lewis. He won an Oscar
for Best Actor in *There Will be Blood* in 2007.

With Henry Winkler (Fonzie).

With Ed Asner (Lou Grant on Mary Tyler Moore Show).

I was on the TV show, Celebrity Circus, (I won the contest).

With Dustin Hoffman at a game.

With basketball legend, Charles Barkley.

With Barbara Eden (I Dream of Jeannie).

With Miss Piggy for a Superbowl Ad.

With Maria Grazia Cucinotta. Maria and I did a film together
called, *Padre Papa*.

With Robert Wagner, Janine Turner (we did *Fatal Error*
together in 1999) and Jill St. John, Robert Wagner's wife.

Me, on *Dancing with The Stars* with my friend Steven Boss (better known as "Twitch") the American dancer and choreographer who has since passed away.

My mom and I with Claudia Cardinali (my Godmother), she worked with my father in an Italian film Certo Certissimo Anzi Probabile (*The Postman*) in 1969. We are laughing because Claudia thought I was my father.

On the show, *Stars in Danger*, I dived from an
Olympic sized diving board and won the singles
diving award.

Chapter 48

SAG (Screen Actors Guild)

In 2019 I found out I had run into problems with the Screen Actors Guild, or SAG, because I made a couple of movies that were not sanctioned by them. This meant the actors and crew in films that I was acting in, at the time, were not in the Screen Actors Guild (Union.)

SAG wrote to me, threatening legal action, which in these terms means that I may not be able to make any SAG sanctioned movies in future, which in fact covers all movies in Hollywood and elsewhere made by actors, directors, producers and even casting agencies working in the film industry in Hollywood. As a result, I now had to deal with this problem.

The issue for me at the time was when I took on a part in a non-SAG production, called *"Santa in Training"* directed by Christian Vogler, I was not earning any money at the time and I was flat broke as a result of being blacklisted while not being represented by the same SAG that was supposed to protect us all in the business.

I was not covered by SAG and I was not receiving any SAG benefits, no health insurance or the financial benefits I had worked hard to get while working in my many SAG sanctioned movies and TV roles over the past thirty years. But because I wasn't getting work, I had lost these benefits. This was a "Catch 22."

Why SAG did nothing to stop the blacklisting for its paid union members, or did nothing to help the actors and actresses, who spoke out against blacklisting which was the very reason I had to take on a part in a non-SAG movie in the first place. Because I was banned from acting in SAG approved movies. Usually, unions represent their members. But this was not so in my case.

I had to pay my bills and I had to find work to prevent filing for bankruptcy. Sorry for that, but the choice to work when I was offered a movie, while I was facing bankruptcy because I was being blacklisted and was told, this is not a union production, was a choice I had to make, due to the circumstances I was forced into. It was a difficult decision for me to take, but my lack of work and the fact that I was looking at filing for bankruptcy meant I had to say yes, I'll do it. Family first.

Where was SAG in helping all of its members to fight against the illegal act of blacklisting in the Hollywood film industry, or are they just part of that club?

Anyway, I had the interview with them which was more like an interrogation comprising other actors who were talking on SAG's behalf and all were against me. They were talking down to me because I was not a famous "A listed" actor like them. I was thinking at the time, what difference does it make if I am an "A list", "B" or "C list?" I still paid my dues and anyway who gets to decide this? We are all in the same business and SAG should treat us all the same when it comes to representation. But they do not, they condone illegal blacklisting and have not stood up for the many actors who had been cast out for not being democrat or socialists.

The result of SAG's actions against me was that I was fined, which, when I cannot work as an actor because I have been blacklisted, (something they have failed to protect) for me and many others, made it difficult for me to pay their fine. But I paid it nevertheless, as I do with everything, I always pay my debts! That was something my father taught me.

Sometimes we all have to make the choice to do what we must, for our family, despite the consequences.

Chapter 49

Life After Hollywood

Things became very difficult for me and my family, which was exactly what those in positions of power in Hollywood wanted for me and my family. The immense and heart wrenching financial difficulties did not come immediately, but rapidly approached with no more movies coming my way, so I had to do something and fast. I had to sell everything I owned, my home and my personal treasures to pay all my debts off.

I then decided to move out of California, away from Hollywood, our home since 1985, more than 30 years, to find a new job to survive and take care of my family. It was tough on my entire family but my faith would get us through.

What Hollywood had done in ending my career, in secret phone calls, amongst the few executives who were once people I considered to be my friends and business colleagues were now not returning calls and I had become a pariah in the same Hollywood I loved worked in for 30 years. So, I took stock of all my talents and decided any job was better than none and I am not a person to sit around feeling sorry for myself. I was fit, I had strength both physical and mental strength and needed to work off my anger at what had happened.

It was in keeping fit, doing my workouts every day, which kept me mentally as well as physically strong to handle whatever came my way. This is something everyone can do and will enable all of you to handle anything that comes your way. I work out as hard now as I did in my 20s (maybe even harder).

Many people in my position after such a major negative event, would be continually looking into the problem. But I was looking at a solution not solely focused on the problem and that was the key for me to move on. I took a job in construction it was the hardest work I had ever done, and I can say to you all that being fit and working out to remain so is something I have always done. Being fit is one thing, but working on construction sites, as I found myself doing, pouring concrete and other things was very tough on my body.

I started work at two in the morning making sure that the job sites I worked at were controlled and supervised by me. I was in the car more than I had ever been before, driving all day long, going to all the work sites each week, nonstop. The work wasn't hard, but the physical demands were something I had never done and each night I was exhausted after work. I can tell you I have the builders and contractors who work on these sites in the highest regard now.

But I also knew that my love was in making movies being in them and perhaps now adding directing and producing, so in addition to my new daytime work I had to keep my hand in by keeping in contact with those who were still my friends. Though they were now fewer they helped me to keep in touch.

Passing Exams

I am proud to say that I did one thing for my mother Yvonne who is highly educated and speaks several languages. She had always been unhappy that because of the many moves we made after emigrating to this country from Italy, when I had not been able to maintain a constant educational focus. I had moved from school to school leaving me with a constantly changing curriculum and lack of any continuity in my education.

As time went on, I became so far behind my classmates that it was embarrassing for me and in and finally, at 15 years old, I dropped out and never took my GED exams. I made the decision to work and not to attend school. I also knew I was so far behind with my knowledge I would have failed my GED if I had taken it at that time. But as I knew from the title of my work out book, I had *"No Excuses"* for not completing my education even now at my age.

So, while I had no film work at all, I went back to school while I was out of Hollywood and completed my GED exam. I can say that this was, for me, a crowning event and I was so proud to have passed. I have to say though the math today is way harder than when I was 15 years old!

I had to study hard to pass the math part of my GED, but I was on a roll so I also went to real estate school and passed my real estate license exam to be able to sell real estate in Florida. I love the real estate business and I enjoy being part of this business. But nevertheless, acting and being in the movie industry is in my blood (thanks papa) so regardless of my additional enterprises I needed to get back in the movie industry.

I can say, once again here, that my faith in God, knowing I had done nothing wrong to justify the situation I and my family now found we in, would carry me through.

Faith can carry anyone through even the most devastating events in their lives. I am proof of this.

Chapter 50

"Grace By Night"

I was slowly digging myself and my family out of the hole that was left after my debacle with Hollywood. I tried my hand at several things in my attempts to get back into the industry I loved but things were tough for me as I was now on the outside looking in. But this would never stop me from starting over and succeeding again as I had several times before.

My first real break in getting back into the movie business came from a script that I had been looking at for some time. It was for a movie titled *Grace By Night,* in which I played the lead role, Jon. I was working with Emma Elle Roberts who played Linda and Shari Rigby who played Claire.

The story line now had a personal meaning for me. *Grace By Night* is about a man trying to face life again following a personal tragedy and I could sure relate to that. I can't explain it, but I felt drawn to make this faith-based Christian movie, since it was about where I was in my life at that time.

I had made a prior faith-based movie titled *One Nation Under God* which also won many awards, and I loved the message of that movie too. It was released at the perfect time when this great nation needed lifting up and the title was perfect with so much negativity going on now in this country.

My latest movie, *Grace By Night* is also a faith-based movie and has appealed to an exceptionally large, and growing, Christian audience. I was executive producer and starred alongside Cameron Arnett and Shari Rigby both of whom shared my values and were wonderful to work with. The back story of making this movie is truly remarkable and shows that unseen forces for good were at work as you will see.

We had not raised the capital we needed to do a big production. But this is where faith and people's Christianity shows itself. Here is where this story becomes very interesting and what happened confirmed my belief that there are truly good people all around us who love to help and will do so willingly. Even without pay as you will see.

We needed extras in many of the scenes, but we had so little funds we couldn't afford to pay them all. We were driving our own cars, buying our own gas, and even paying for our own hotel and living expenses. There was no lunch cart as there normally is while filming and the young people who worked with us included school kids who were happy to work with us while doing their homework on the set while working without pay. Meghan Leigh Leon, who co-produced it and assisted with the screen play was also incredible to work with.

We filmed a good portion of the movie in Thompson High School in Birmingham, Alabama and those kids were awesome to work with. There was nothing they couldn't do to help make the movie a success to create. The atmosphere on the set was electric with everyone, and I mean everyone, from the director, the cameraman, actors, extras, everyone working together doing whatever needed to be done and it was one of the best sets I have ever worked on.

It was as if an unseen force was working through the spirit of all who were creating that movie. We all felt the spiritual presence helping us to succeed, under the meagre budget we were able to put together and, believe it or not, we came in under budget! I can promise you all, to come in under budget, just never happens!

I want to also mention an extraordinary talent who I worked with William (Will) Oliver who played Calvin in the movie. He and I became good friends and I know he will go far in the movie industry. Making this movie was like a dream come true I was back on my game doing what I love to do, and I acted my role from my heart because this movie was very close to what had happened to me and the redemption that can follow a fall.

So far, even before the official release, which is set for 2024 our movie has won several awards, including, *Best Picture Angel Award,* in the 2023 ICFF (International Christian Film Festival) awards. I won the *Angel Award for Best Actor* in a feature film for this film. There were 1000 entrants for the festival and *Grace By Night* has been nominated for 9 awards and won the Movie Guide 2019 Kairos Prize for "Most Inspirational Screenplay."

As well as the other awards it has been officially nominated for the Christian World View Awards for Featured Films section and had been placed at the top of the list of nominations. I was so happy that my production has the recognition I felt it deserved.

When Katia and I watched the movie, we were moved by what we saw and we both loved how the final completed movie was presented. After that showing the movie got a standing ovation which further convinced me we had made a truly great movie!

I knew that this was a new me and I know I will continue to make movies and I will love doing so, after all it's in my blood and I have never ever backed down to bullies!

Sometimes at our lowest point something will happen to lift us up once again, as was this case for me.

Chapter 51

Where to From Here

Moving On

I hope that on reading all that my family and I have been through, our lives in two beautiful countries, Czechoslovakia then Italy, and the decisions we made in order to live a better life. Now, with the release of my book, it sheds light on my determination and inner strength which I have relied on over and over again enabling me to pick myself up and start again.

We learned that my grandmother was murdered in Prague, we lost my great grandparents in Auschwitz, my father lost his career as a well-known actor in Italy. These things happened because of circumstances far outside our control. After each situation we had to re-invent ourselves, as we did moving here in America.

I hope also that the impression you have on reading my book is that I have a close, loving family who want the same things that you and all families want, to earn money and to live our lives in safety, prosperity and in the pursuit of happiness. My family had the resilience to withstand the extraordinary events that have surrounded our past in events we could not control. We all have the ability to pick ourselves up after every fall, whether it's a big fall or a small one doesn't really matter.

What does matter is that we all do, in fact, keep on picking ourselves up, in order to move on. From my own personal experiences, I have seen and suffered from hate and there is no room for hate in our lives. Hate stems from fear. Fear and lies are the darkness that surrounds us all when we don't allow others to hold their own beliefs and views.

What is going on in the Hollywood movie industry right now has little to do with making movies but everything to do with power. The power of the few to decide, like cowards, behind closed doors, deciding on who will work and who will not. This is naturally based in part on their popularity but also on their fit for a particular role and certainly should never be based on their political views or opinions.

Is this not against freedom of speech, freedom to work and to have the same rules for all? But I can say, in hindsight, that to state a political viewpoint, in this day can and will affect your future especially if your view does not agree with those in power. We as a country have moved away from what our founding fathers envisioned.

There are millions of fans who would pay over and over to see the performances in upcoming movies with movie stars they love to watch simply because they have played the rolls they chose in their movies and entertained us all. But one thing I learned is that stating our beliefs on religion or politics can have severe consequences.

The power to abuse young and upcoming actresses is part of the evil side of Hollywood and to wield this power in such a way should never be acceptable in the country that is supposed to show the entire world what America represents, freedom and justice for all. They do not represent the beautiful industry they are in.

The silent majority, who agree with me, should help to stop this and collectively choose not be part of the problem by condoning it with their silence. The few, who hate and are in positions of power in Hollywood and have the power to tell lies about actors and actresses, to an ever willing and biased press, preventing them from ever working again.

Then there is the silent majority who only want to make films, be in films and let the entertainment industry be all that it can be, could be a power for good and help change this corruption. They have the power to do this if they all decide to make a change.

My passion and determination to get up each time I fall or am smacked down has made me finally speak out and I have done so loud and clear, here in this book which is the truth about my life so far.

I am proof that hard work does pay off. I have also made the choice to speak out and ask others to do the same, to speak out against hate, in all its forms, especially as it is now so prevalent in the world.

As I said back then in 2016, when I addressed the Republican National Committee, where all this began, America needs to have unity not division and this is even more true today."

As I finished my book, there was a pandemic, a virus the Corona Virus, or COVID 19 and from what I can see, many countries were working together to share information to find a vaccine to cure this. This is the kind of unity I was talking about in my presentation in 2016, but now it seems to be even more important to save thousands, if not millions of lives around the world. Now it crosses the borders of many countries that are sharing data to help one another in a global time of mutual need to save humanity.

All countries can and should work closer together, not against each other, as love is always stronger than hate. Utopian? maybe, but unless we have inspired dreams, based on knowledge and truth, we have nothing to strive for.

A Tribute to My Papa

As the result of the terrible Covid19 outbreak, my father (Papa), succumbed and passed away in an LA hospital. After going round in circles trying to find and call whoever was responsible to make a video call happen between my father and my family. My sister Simonne and I were finally able to have video calls with our dad. Simonne was on the West Coast and I was in Florida.

The hospital staff would not allow my sister or me to visit our dad not even if we were wearing fully protective clothing. I have no idea why this was so damn impossible to achieve but it was. We called him as often as possible but we could see he was in bad shape and getting worse day by day. On the last call we had with him he could hardly breathe but he managed to wink at us both to let us know he could see us both which we will treasure always. I should add here that the hospital lost his wallet and his belongings and we were never able to recover these personal items.

I learned many things from my Papa many things, not the least of which was the way he was always with me when I needed him and at the times when I needed his strength and knowledge, not only in the movie business, but when I needed a father figure to guide me. He always looked good no matter what he was doing and he always took good care of himself. This is something I too will always do no matter what. The things he taught me which I will always keep with me no matter what. These were his values, family always comes first, he had a passion and a drive to succeed and he did succeed in everything he did.

Papa loved racing and this he passed on to me and is something I will spend a lot more time with because I love everything about the sport too. Papa also had to deal with the loss of his family and losing his own father at just 15, dying in his arms was a terrible thing for a 15-year-old.

He, like me, had to keep going, keeping our heads above water and together with our mother Yvonne, they succeeded in keeping the bad side of life away from us while we were young. That awful fire in Rome where we lost everything, my papa and my mother kept the truth from us for many years. That was their strength.

He also dealt with the movie industry grinding to a halt around him yet he was prepared to start again in a foreign country, not knowing the language and knowing very few people here. We will treasure his life as part of our own and we know his spirit will always be with us, always!

And Finally

I hope you have all enjoyed reading about me and my family, our lives, seeing he events that have happened and have shaped us, looking through our eyes, seeing all we have been through as a family. These are the ups and downs of family life and happen to many of us. I wrote my book also as an inspiration to others, for you my readers and especially for young people, many of whom need inspiration these days to stay focused on their dreams as I had to.

I continue to work out each and every day, I have a rigorous program that no matter what and regardless of what is going on around me. This is my way of life and will never change. There is also the fact that I love the vibe of a tough work out. It keeps me in shape both mentally and physically. If you are not doing it, trust me it will improve your life.

If I could dream of being in movies in Hollywood, from where I was living in Rome, Italy, or dream of driving a race car on the world-famous Indianapolis Motor Speedway and achieve these dreams, then so can you! But first, you have to dream your dream, then decide to make it happen. As someone once said, "Any man can do what another has done."

Many of the people whose paths have crossed mine also have incredible stories to tell, but this is my family's story and I want to leave all my readers with this thought; that any of you, no matter how many times you are knocked down, have the ability to get back up and become successful. It's the math of "plus one." If you can pick yourself up one more time than you fall you will always succeed.

I was able to get through all that happened to me because I placed my trust in God to help me get through. I have already picked myself up and, with God's help, I will be back in the movie business that I love, as I am doing now. But the difference is that now I will be back in the world I love, making movies, together with the many friends who stood by me, friends who were there for me in those difficult times and we will not allow those who hate to affect us.

I also searched for love in each of my relationships and finally found the one person, Katia, who I am with now who has helped me get through these very tough times and without her love, affection and support, being there for me, I may not have made it through.

I am now writing, producing, directing and starring in my own movies, movies that allow me to really act and show my true abilities. I hope you will love to watch my future work knowing that politics will have no place in what we are doing!

Our next book, "Yvonne," will be about my mother Yvonne and all she had to go through from the age of three living in Prague, as a three-year old acrobat. Then as an eight-year-old child hostage, as a singer also and being on stage in lands very foreign and very different to America she too succeeded.

Many of us can choose how we live our lives and we can choose to pick ourselves up and move on from anything bad that happens in our lives and bad things will always happen, it's part of life. We also have the choice not to be part of the silent majority when we see evil which is then allowed to flourish by those who do nothing to prevent it. I am not one of those and although it cost me everything, it showed me the true value of who I am and I will always stand up for what I believe is right and do the things that make me and my family happy.

So, for me, Antonio Sabato Jr. I can tell you all, no matter what, the best is yet to come!

With love,

Antonio Sabato Jr.

Antonio Sabato Jr.
Awards
and
Nominations

Beverly Hills Film Festival

2009	**Winner** Best Male Performance	Drifter: Henry Lee Lucas (2009)

Christian Film Festival-Menchville Baptist Church

2018	**Winner** Best Supporting Actor	One Nation Under God (2020) Shared with: - Casper Van Dien - Robert Belushi - Herschel Walker
	Winner Best Actor Supporting Fan Favorite	One Nation Under God (2020)

Image Awards (NAACP)

2007	**Nominee** Image Award	Outstanding Actor in a Daytime Drama Series: The Bold and the Beautiful (1987)
2006	**Nominee** Image Award	Outstanding Actor in a Daytime Drama Series: The Bold and the Beautiful (1987)

<u>1994</u>	**Nominee** Soap Opera Digest Award	Hottest Male Star: <u>General Hospital</u>
<u>1993</u>	**Nominee** Soap Opera Digest Award	Outstanding Male Newcomer <u>General Hospital</u> Hottest Male Star: <u>General Hospital</u>

My roles in Films TV and Reality Shows

"Love Will Never Do (Without You)"	Extra	1990	Music video for Janet Jackson
agazzo delle mani d'acciaio Karate Rock	Kevin Foster	1990	Italian film
Fuga da Kayenta Arizona Road	Emiliano	1991	Italian film
E se non avessi amore	Pier Giorgio Frassati (	1991	Italian film
E non avessi l'amore	Pier Giorgio Frassati	1991	Italian film
General Hospital	Jagger Cates	1992-1995	Series
Moment of Truth: Why My Daughter?	A.J. Treece	1993	TV film
Jailbreakers	Tony	1994	TV film
Earth 2	Alonzo Solace	1994-1995	TV show
Melrose Place	Jack Perezi	1995	7 episodes
Her Hidden Truth	Detective Matt Samoni	1995	TV film
If Looks Could Kill	John Hawkins	1996	TV film
Padre papà [italian]	Don Giuseppe	1996	Mini series
Thrill	Jack Colson	1996	TV film
Code Name: Wolverine	Harry Gordini / Wolverine	1996	TV film
Lois & Clark: The New Adventures of Superman	Bob Stanford / Deathstroke	1996	TV show
Happily Ever After: Fairy Tales for Every Child	Mario	1997	Episode: Thumbelina
High Voltage	Johnny Clay	1997	Movie
The Perfect Getaway	Randy Savino	1998	TV film
Circle	Jeremy Bonner	1998	TV Film
The Big Hit	Vince	1998	Movie
Tribe	Jack Osborne	1999	4 episodes
Fatal Error	Dr. Nick Baldwin	1999	TV film

My Roles in Films TV and Reality Shows Cont.:

Tribe	Jack Osborne	1999	4 episodes
Goosed	Dr. Steven Stevenson	1999	TV Film
Wasteland	Jack	1999	Episode: Double Date
The Outer Limits	Chad Warner / Sid Camden	2000	Episode: Skin Deep
The Chaos Factor	Jack Poynt	2000	
Charmed	Bane Jessup	2000	2 episodes
Vola Sciusciù	Tony	2000	TV film
Guilty as Charged	Sergeant Hawks	2000	TV film
Final Ascent	David	2000	TV film
Mindstorm	Dan Oliver	2001	TV film
Shark Hunter	Spencer Northcut	2001	TV film
Longshot	Tommy Sutton	2001	TV film
Hyper Sonic	Grant Irvine	2002	TV film
Seconds to Spare	Paul Blake	2002	TV film
Dead Above Ground	Sergeant Dan DeSousa	2002	TV film
See Jane Date	Timothy Rommelly	2003	TV film
Wasabi Tuna	Fredrico	2003	
Bugs	Matt Pollack	2003	TV film
Testosterone	Pablo Alesandro	2003	film
Half & Half	Carlo	2004	Episode: The Big Double Date with My Mate Episode
Becker	Linda's boyfriend	2004	Episode: DNR
The Help	Dwayne	2004	7 episodes
Joey	Kyle	2005	Episode: Joey and the Tonight Show
Jane Doe: Til Death Do Us Part	Joey Angelini	2005	TV film
Crash Landing	Major John Masters	2005	film
The Bold and the Beautiful	Dante Damiano	2005-2006	series
But Can They Sing?	Himself	2005	Reality TV show
Deadly Skies	Richard Donovan	2006	TV film
Reckless Behavior: Caught on Tape	Greg Vlasi	2007	TV film
Destination: Infestation	Ethan Hart	2007	TV film
Bad Girl Island	Michael Pace	2007	TV film
Ghost Voyage	Michael	2008	TV film
General Hospital: Night Shift	Jagger Cates	2008	14 episodes
NCIS	Dale Kapp	2008	Episode: Road Kill

My roles in Films TV and Reality Shows Cont.

Drifter: Henry Lee Lucas	Henry Lee Lucas	2009	Film
Ugly Betty	Himself	2009	Episode: The Fall Issue
Scrubs	Himself	2009	Episode: Our Drunk Friend
Princess of Mars	John Carter	2009	
My Antonio	Himself	2009	Reality TV show
Celebrity Circus	Himself / Contestant	2009	Reality TV show
CSI: NY	Davi Santos	2010	Episode: The Formula
The Tonight Show with Jay Leno	Ross Matthews	2010	Episode: #18.89
Rizzoli & Isles	Jorge	2010	Episode: I Kissed A Girl
Bones	Terror	2010	Episode: The Maggots in the Meathead
Balls to the Wall	Sven	2011	
God Reschedules Rapture		2011	Short film
Hot in Cleveland	Leandro	2011	Episode: Dancing Queens
Secrets from Her Past	Dr. Shawn Tessle	2011	TV film
Celebrity Wife Swap	Himself	2012	Seires
The Three Stooges	Handsome Guy #1	2012	TV Film
Little Women, Big Cars	A.J.	2012	TV Series
Little Women, Big Cars 2	A.J.	2012	TV Series
Femme Fatales	Bart	2012	Episode: Gun Twisted
Baby Daddy	Gerard	2013	Episode: All's Flair in Love and War
Castle	Ramon Russo	2013	Episode: Need to Know
The League	Father Zaragosa	2013	2 episodes
Hell's Kitchen	Himself	2013	Episode: "5 Chefs Compete Part 3"
All I Want for Christmas	Mike Patterson	2014	TV film
Fix It and Finish It	Himself / Host	2014	TV Series
Intikam	Varol	2015	TV Film

My roles in Films TV and Reality Shows Cont.

Hometown Hero	Jason	2016	TV film
Dance Night Obsession	Miguel	2016	TV Film
Dark Paradise	Dario	2016	TV film
The Encounter	Dr. Max Huber	2016	Episode: Just Believe
Inspired to Kill	Paul	2017	TV film
Malibu Dan the Family Man	Frane Calloway	2017	Episode: Filthy Poor
Hilton Head Island	Jude Trisk	2017	Episode: Genesis
Antonio: Down Under	Antonio	2017	TV mini-series
One Nation Under God	Senator Viera	2019	Film
Santa In Training	Eddie	2019	TV Film
Grace By Night	Jon	2019	film
God's Not Dead-We The People	Mike McKinnon	2021	Film
Carolina's Calling	Martin Haas	2021	film

Biography of co-author Tony Moore

Tony Moore is an author with 7 books published, and with 6 more that he contributed to publishing. He is an entrepreneur and holds an engineering degree. His books include, *"One of A Kind Making Things Happen,"* his motivational autobiography. Tony's freelance writing includes many published articles for business journals as well as an inclusion in Emeritus Professor  Malcolm Mc. Donald's 47th book titled, *"Strategic Planning."* This book is a business publication and is part of the curriculum as required reading for students taking a 4-year MBA degree.

After moving from London to Brussels, Belgium, Tony launched a successful global business, into 30 countries for a Fortune 500 Swedish company. After moving to the U.S.A., he became GM of a 90-year-old failing U.S. technical glove manufacturing company. He took that company into LEAN manufacturing, the first U.S. glove company to do so, and took it to becoming the biggest glove manufacturing company in the USA.

Tony was also part of the U.S. Army's "Rapid Field Initiative" in a military technical committee designing specialized gloves for the U.S. Army. He designed and built several gloves for the U.S. Army one of which is now in every U.S. GI's kitbag. He also worked with US firefighting service where one of his gloves became one of the biggest selling, NFPA certified firefighting gloves, in the U.S. and is currently widely used by many major fire departments here.

Tony has launched several companies including a fragrance company with the former "Nose" of Elizabeth Arden. Their fragrance, *"Stardust,"* was launched in the prestigious Bergdorf Goodman in New York and was featured in Marc Rosen's book "Glamor Icons," which was featured in an exhibition in London's famous Somerset House. Tony was also featured on a Fox News business program, *"Inspirational Entrepreneurs."* Tony has been on many other radio interviews and podcasts both as an author and as an entrepreneur. He was also US. Correspondent for a UK radio station with his many interviews now on his YouTube channel along with his podcasts.

 Tony is presently a professional writer and co-founder of Briton Publishing LLC. He lives in Indianapolis with his wife Sue and sons Nicholas and James. He also has two daughters Amanda and Georgia, living in Ealing, West London along with his six grandchildren.